OUR WORLD WORKBOOK LEVEL 3

NATIONAL GEOGRAPHIC

OUR WORLD

SERIES EDITORS
Joan Kang Shin
JoAnn (Jodi) Crandall

AUTHOR
Lesley Ito

NATIONAL GEOGRAPHIC LEARNING | CENGAGE Learning

Australia • Brazil • Japan • Korea • Mexico • Singapore • Spain • United Kingdom • United States

Unit 0

1 **Listen and read.** Match the questions to the answers. Draw lines. **TR: 02**

1. How do you spell *eraser*?
2. What's the difference between *on* and *in*?
3. How do you say *lápiz* in English?
4. I don't understand. Can you help me, please?
5. Could you repeat that, please?

a. I can show you.

b. Yes, sure.

c. It's a *pencil.*

d. e-r-a-s-e-r

e. Sure, e-r-a-s-e-r.

2 **Listen and circle.** **TR: 03**

1. 27 + 20 =	27 - 20 =
2. 101 + 35 =	101 - 35 =
3. 1,000,000	1,000,000,000
4. 1,000,000,000	1,000,000
5. 17th	7th
6. 2nd	3rd

3 **Do the puzzle.** Unscramble the words. Write one letter in each square.

Seasons and Months

UMESMR	□	□	□	□	□ 2	□			
WNTIER	□ 1	□	□	□ 8	□	□			
REBTOCO	□ 9	□ 13	□	□ 10	□	□ 7	□		
RUFREYBA	□	□	□	□	□ 11	□	□	□	
PRNIGS	□ 16	□	□ 12	□	□	□			
TESBPMEER	□ 17	□	□	□	□	□ 6	□	□	□
CAHMR	□	□ 15	□	□ 4	□				
BENREOVM	□	□ 5	□	□	□	□	□	□	
LFAL	□	□	□ 3	□ 14					

4 **Find and write.** Look at Activity 3. Find the letters above the numbers. Write the letters above the same numbers in the squares below. Then read the message.

W	□	□	□	□	□	□		□	□		□	□	□		□	□	□	□	□	!
1	2	3	4	5	6	7		8	9		10	11	12		13	14	15	16	17	

5 **Look, read, and write.** Use words from the box.

hers	his	mine	ours	yours	theirs

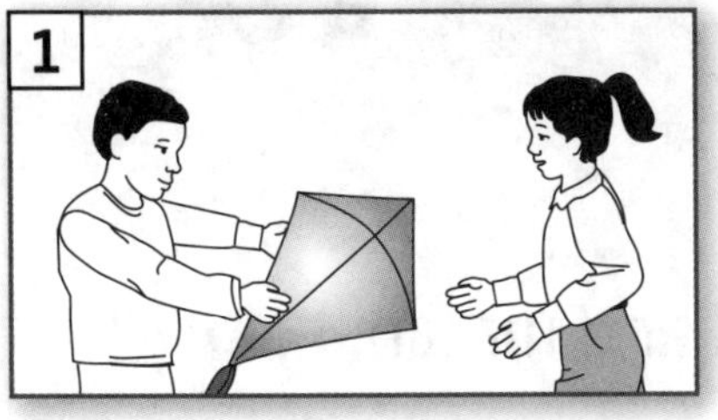

1. The kite is ______.
2. The kite is ______.
3. The kite is ______.
4. The kite is ______.

6 **Read.** Circle the correct answer.

1. Where's my hat? Oh, I see ____!
   a. me b. it c. them
2. Where's my sister? I can't see ____.
   a. you b. him c. her
3. I want a cookie. Can you give ____ a cookie, please?
   a. me b. us c. them
4. I like my friends. I like to play with ____.
   a. you b. me c. them
5. Do you see my brother? I can't see ____.
   a. you b. him c. her
6. Hello, Alex and Maria! I have cookies for ____.
   a. them b. you c. it
7. My friends and I want to play a board game. You can play with ____!
   a. us b. them c. you

Unit 1

A Helping Hand

1 **Listen and write.** Then listen again. Read and match. **TR: 04**

hold hands	teach	hug	feed	protect
take care of	help	give	carry	pick up

1. I ______________ my grandmother. ☐

2. I ______________ my goldfish. ☐

3. A mother can ______________ her baby. ☐

4. I ______________ my mother. ☐

5. I ______________ the baby. ☐

6. I ______________ my brother the ABCs. ☐

a

b

c

d

e

f

7. I ________________ with my friend. ☐

8. I ________________ the hamster. ☐

9. I ________________ my bird. ☐

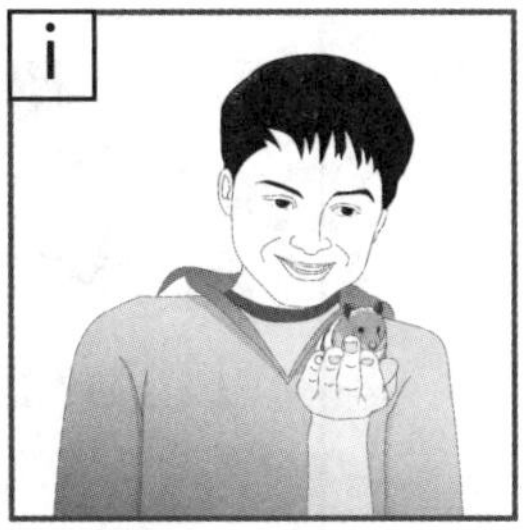

10. I ________________ my pet a bath. ☐

2 Read and write.

I like to ____.

I like to ____.

I like to ____.

3 **Work with a partner.** Ask and answer.

Do you like to help your grandmother?

Yes, I do.

4 **Listen to the song.** Look. Number the pictures. **TR: 05**

5 **Look, read, and circle.** Look at the pictures in Activity 4. Read and circle the correct word.

1. I have to hold hands with my **grandmother / grandfather**.
2. I have to wash my **goat / goldfish**.
3. I have to comb my **cat / bird**.
4. I have to teach my **sisters / brothers** their 1, 2, 3s.
5. I have to pick up my **dog / frog**.
6. I have to carry my family's new **baby / horse**.
7. I have to read to my **sister / brother**.
8. I have to feed my **dog / snake**.

GRAMMAR

What does he do **before** breakfast? He feeds his dog **before** breakfast.

What does he do **after** breakfast? He brushes his teeth **after** breakfast.

6 **Unscramble.** Write.

1. What does he do before school?
   washes / his / face / He
   ____
2. does / after / What / do / he / school
   ____
   He helps his mother.
3. breakfast / What / do / before / she / does
   ____
   She brushes her teeth.
4. What does she do before school?
   feeds / hamster / her / She
   ____

7 **Listen.** Match. Draw lines. **TR: 06**

1. What do you do after school?
2. What do you do before breakfast?
3. What do you do after breakfast?
4. What do you do before school?

a. I hug my grandmother.
b. I feed my cat.
c. I help my mother.
d. I take care of my brother.

8 **What do you do?** Draw and write.

This is me. I ________________ before breakfast. I ________________ after breakfast. I ________________ before school. I ________________ after school.

I like ________________.

9 **Work with a partner.** Draw your partner. Write about your partner.

This is ________________. He/She ________________ before breakfast. He/She ________________ after breakfast. He/She ________________ after school.

10 Listen and write. TR: 07

feed my cat   have a snack   make my bed   take a shower

1. I ______________________ before breakfast.
2. I ______________________ after breakfast.
3. I ______________________ before school.
4. I ______________________ after school.

11 Look. Read and match.

1. He takes a shower at seven thirty.
2. He makes his bed at eight o'clock.
3. He walks to school at eight fifteen.
4. He comes home at three forty-five.
5. He eats a snack at four o'clock.
6. He does his homework at four twenty.

12 Work with a partner. Ask and answer.

When does he take a shower?

He takes a shower at seven thirty.

GRAMMAR

	M	T	W	T	F
Omar **never** eats breakfast at 6:00.					
Omar **sometimes** eats breakfast at 6:30.		✓			✓
Omar **usually** eats breakfast at 7:00.	✓		✓	✓	
Omar **always** walks to school at 7:30.	✓	✓	✓	✓	✓

13 **Listen.** Draw lines to match. **TR: 08**

1. She	always	helps at home	at 3:15.
2. She	usually	has a snack	at 3:45.
3. He	usually	takes a shower	at 4:45.
4. She	sometimes	does her homework	at 5:30.
5. He	sometimes	makes his bed	at 6:30.
6. He	never	comes home	at 8:00.

14 **What about you?** Write about when you do things.

1. I ___always___ eat breakfast at ___7:00___.
2. I ________ make my bed at ______.
3. I ________ eat lunch at ______.
4. I ________ have a snack at ______.
5. I ________ come home at ______.
6. I ________ do my homework at ______.

always
never
sometimes
usually

15 **Work with a partner.** Student 1, go to page 118. Student 2, go to page 120. Take turns.

16 **Do the puzzle.** Read the sentences. Unscramble the words.

1. 

It's four T W (E) N T Y (TTWYNE).

2. I _______ (LLSYAUU) drink milk for breakfast, but today I drank juice.

3. I ______ (SAAWYL) wake up early.

4. I _____ (NEEVR) get to school late. I'm always on time.

5. 

It's eleven ______ (RIYTHT).

6. He _____ (SAEKT) a shower in the morning.

7. I never eat a _____ (KCSAN) after school.

8. I brush my teeth _____ (REATF) breakfast.

9. I _______ (PERTOTC) my pet from wild animals.

17 **Answer the riddle.** Unscramble the circled letters in the puzzle to solve the riddle.

This animal is gray and has a long trunk. It's very big and can live to be seventy years old. African ones have big ears, and Asian ones have small ears. What animal is it?

(E) ( ) ( ) ( ) ( ) ( ) ( ) ( )

18 **Listen and read.** Can you say these fast? **TR: 09**

1. I slurp snacks and sodas at six sixteen.
2. Meena makes many milkshakes in the morning.
3. Before four, fix the fifteenth flower vase.

19 **Listen and read.** TR: 10

The Daily Lives of Animals

What do you do every day? Most kids wake up in the morning, eat three or four meals a day, help their families, and go to sleep at night. Many animals don't live the same way kids do. They sleep in the daytime or eat only at night. Some animals never sleep! They take care of babies in different ways.

The red-necked nightjar is a bird from Spain and northern Africa. It flies in the evening and eats insects. It sleeps on the ground during the day. Most birds lay eggs in a nest, but this bird lays eggs on the ground!

The koala lives in Australia. It only eats eucalyptus tree leaves at night. The koala sleeps in the morning, afternoon, and evening. It sleeps more than fifteen hours a day! It has a small baby that grows in its mother's pouch.

The great white shark lives in oceans all over the world. The great white shark never stops swimming. It always eats and never sleeps. The mother doesn't take care of its babies. The babies swim away from their hungry mother!

Red-necked nightjar

Koala pouch

Great white shark

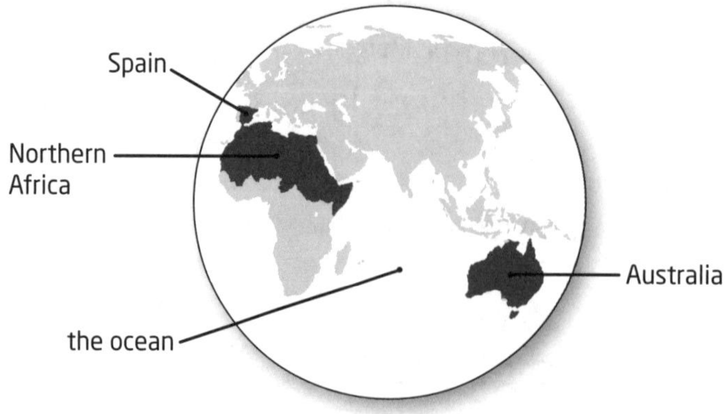

Weird but true **Many sharks are small. The smallest shark is the size of a man's hand!**

20 **Read.** Check **T** for *True* and **F** for *False*.

1. The koala sleeps more than fifteen hours a day. Ⓣ Ⓕ
2. The red-necked nightjar sleeps in a tree. Ⓣ Ⓕ
3. A great white shark takes care of her babies. Ⓣ Ⓕ
4. The great white shark always swims. Ⓣ Ⓕ
5. The red-necked nightjar lives in Australia. Ⓣ Ⓕ
6. The koala eats insects in the evening. Ⓣ Ⓕ

21 **Look and read.** Fill in the chart.

animal	sleeps	eats	takes care of babies
		eats eucalyptus leaves at night	baby koala grows in its mother's pouch
red-necked nightjar		eats insects in the evening	lays eggs on the ground, not in a nest
			never takes care of its babies

22 **Read and write.**

1. When do koalas eat?

____

2. Where does a baby koala grow?

____

3. When do sharks take care of their babies?

____

4. Where do red-necked nightjars lay their eggs?

____

23 **Read.** Read the letter from Sara. She uses *first, before,* and *after* to tell the order that she does things. Circle the words *first, before,* and *after* in the letter.

Dear Eva,

I have a pet dog. His name is Fluff. I always take care of my dog before I go to school. First, I feed my dog. I play with Fluff after he eats. After school, I take Fluff for a walk. Sometimes I give my dog a bath!

Your friend,

Sara

24 **Choose a friend.** Write about your friend's day. Tell the order your friend does things. Use words from the box.

first	always	usually	sometimes	never
before breakfast	after breakfast	before school	after school	

____

____

____

____

____

____

25 **Work with a partner.** Play a game. Write in the tic-tac-toe board about your day. Read the sentences and play tic-tac-toe.

I usually ____________ in the afternoon.	I wake up at ____________.	I ____________ feed my goldfish before school.
I go to bed at ____________.	I ____________ play video games in the morning.	I sometimes ____________ at 3:00.
I ____________ play soccer after school.	I usually ____________ at 7:00.	I ____________ take care of my pet.

26 **Read and write.**

1. Does a hamster usually take a shower?

   A hamster never takes a shower.

2. Does a goldfish somctimes have a snack?

   ____

3. Do you sometimes hold hands with your friends?

   ____

4. What time do you usually eat breakfast?

   ____

5. What do you sometimes do after lunch?

   ____

6. What do you always like to do?

   ____

Unit 2

My Place in the World

1 **Look and write.**

2 Listen and match. Write the letter in the box. TR: 11

3 **Listen to the song.** Write. TR: 12

Where are the post office, the ________________,

the supermarket, and the park?

Where's the ________________?

Where's the library?

Where are the zoo, the ________________, and a

swimming pool?

Here's the post office, the toy store,

the supermarket, and the ________________.

Here's the bakery, the library, the zoo, the school,

a swimming pool, and a ________________, too!

4 **Write a new verse for the song.** Write questions about places in your town.

Where are ________________ and ________________?

Where's the ________________?

Where's the ________________?

Where are ________________ and ________________?

GRAMMAR

Can you **help** me?	Sure. **How can I help?**
Where's the museum?	It's **on** Main Street.
	It's **next to** the police station.
	It's **across from** the bakery.
	It's **on the corner of** Main Street **and** First Street.
	It's **behind** the movie theater.
	It's **between** the park **and** the school.

5 Listen and match. TR: 13

1. Can you help me?
   Sure. How can I help?
   Where's the supermarket? ___
2. Can you help me?
   Sure. How can I help?
   Where's the post office? ___
3. Can you help me?
   Sure. How can I help?
   Where's the restaurant? ___
4. Can you help me?
   Sure. How can I help?
   Where's the hospital? ___
5. Can you help me?
   Sure. How can I help?
   Where's the drug store? ___

a. It's between the toy store and the park.

b. It's across from the bakery.

c. It's on the corner of Main Street and First Street.

d. It's behind the movie theater.

e. It's next to the museum.

6 **Draw and write.** Draw some buildings on this map of an imaginary town. Label your map.

hospital	park	supermarket	museum	bakery
post office	school	movie theater	police station	
drug store	train station	toy store	restaurant	

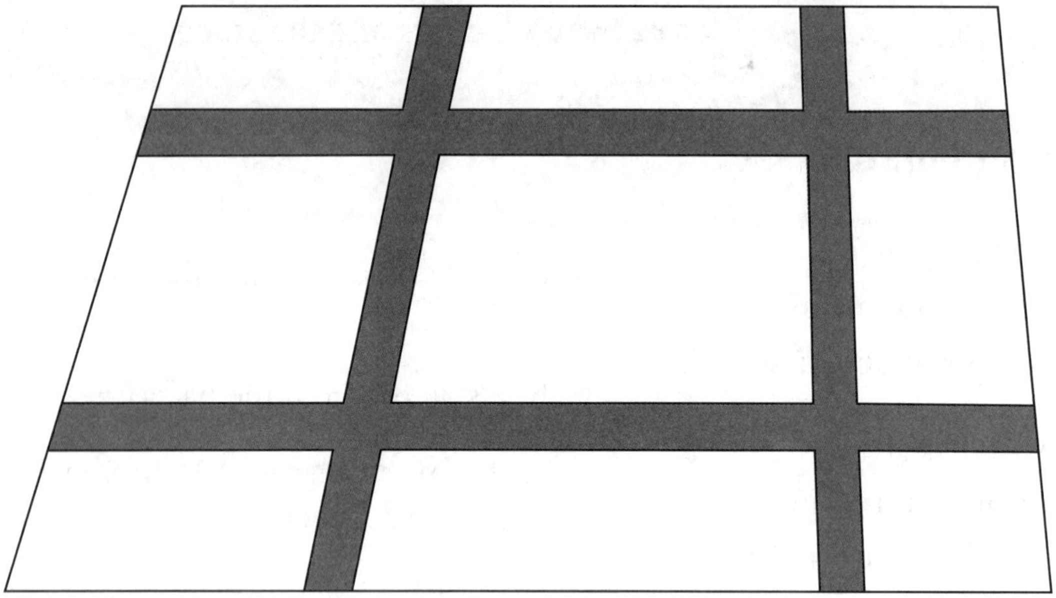

7 **Look and write.** Use your map from Activity 6. Write about where things are.

1. Can you ________ me?
   Sure. How ________ I help?
   Where's the ____________?
   The ____________ is ____________.

2. ________ you help me?
   Sure. ________ can I help?
   Where's the ____________?
   The ____________ is ____________.

3. ________ you help me?
   Sure. How ________ I help?
   ________ the ____________?
   The ____________ is ____________.

4. ________ you help me?
   Sure. How ________ I help?
   ________ the ____________?
   The ____________ is ____________.

8 Look and write.

a mall   a swimming pool   a zoo   a stadium   a library

____

____

____

____

____

9 Listen. Circle the answers. TR: 14

1. She wants to go to the **swimming pool / stadium.** She wants to **see her favorite baseball team / buy some shoes.**
2. I want to go to the **library / mall.** I want to **play in the water / study.**
3. He wants to go to the **zoo / mall.** He wants to **buy some new shoes / see the hippos.**
4. She wants to go to the **swimming pool / stadium.** She wants to **see her favorite baseball team / play in the water.**
5. I want to go to the **zoo / mall.** I love the **elephants / movies**!

GRAMMAR

How can I get to the supermarket?

Go straight ↑.
Turn right → on White Street.
Turn left ← on Second Street.

10 **Look at the map.** Write.

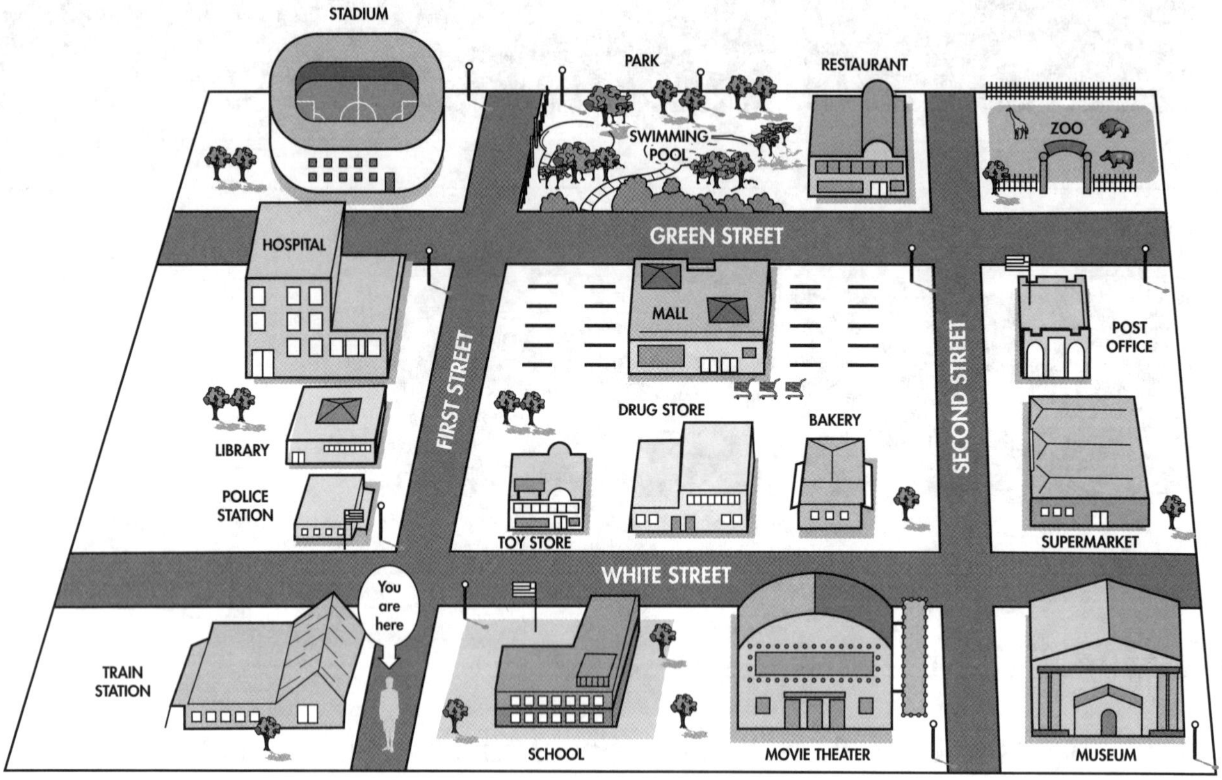

1. How can I get to the stadium?

   Go __________ on First Street. Turn __________ on Green Street. It's on the corner of ______________ and ______________.

2. How can I get to the post office?

   Go __________ on First Street. Turn __________ on Green Street. It's __________ the zoo.

11 **Work with a partner.** Student 1, go to page 119. Student 2, go to page 121.

12 **Play a board game.** Play with a partner. Put your erasers on START. Use a coin. Heads = one space. Tails = two spaces. Say where you are. The first person to get HOME is the winner!

Where are you now?

I'm at school.

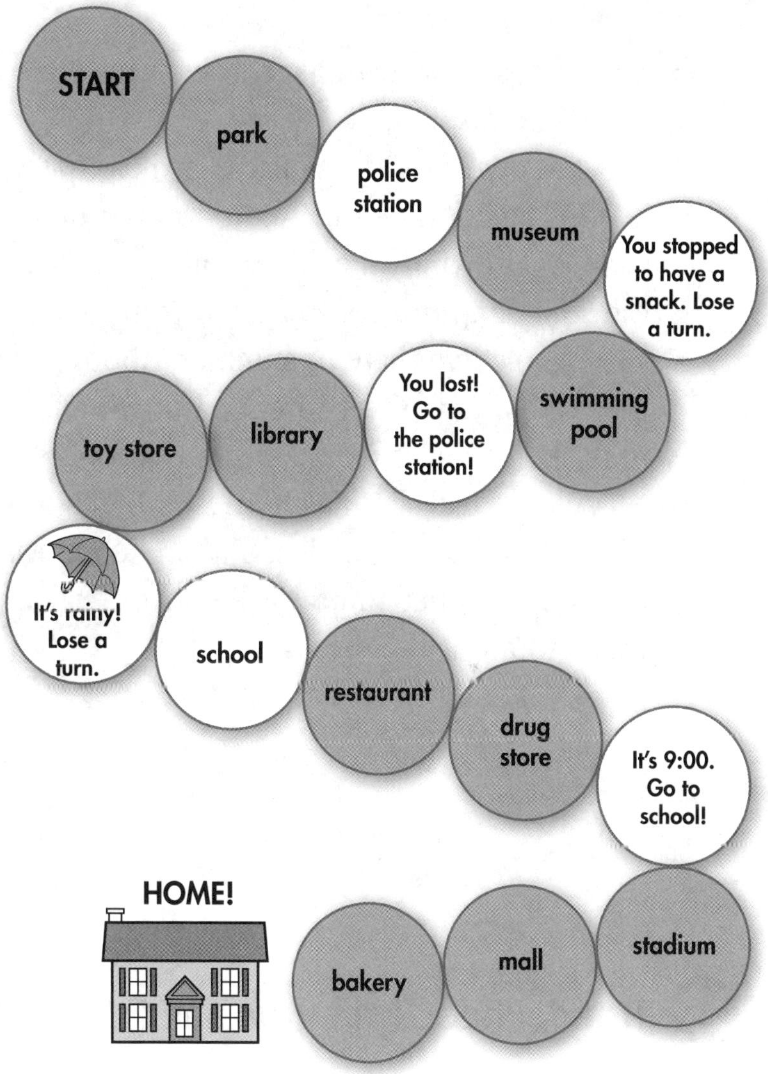

13 **Listen and read.** Can you say these fast? **TR: 15**

1. A supermarket sells salty shellfish.
2. Bill is busy at the bookstore buying big blue books.
3. Lisa looks right at the library.

14 Listen and read. TR: 16

Villa las Estrellas – A Town in Antarctica

What is your town like? Does it have a school? A post office? A hospital?

The town of Villa las Estrellas has those places, too, and it is in the continent of Antarctica! Antarctica is very cold, snowy, and windy. People usually live in Antarctica only for the summer, but they live all year in Villa las Estrellas. About 150 people live there in summer. About seventy people live there in winter. Nights are long in winter. The sun shines only four or five hours a day. The sun always shines in summer.

Villa las Estrellas has houses, a bank, a school, a hospital, small stores, a post office, and a church. Many people come to visit. They like to go to the post office and send letters from Antarctica!

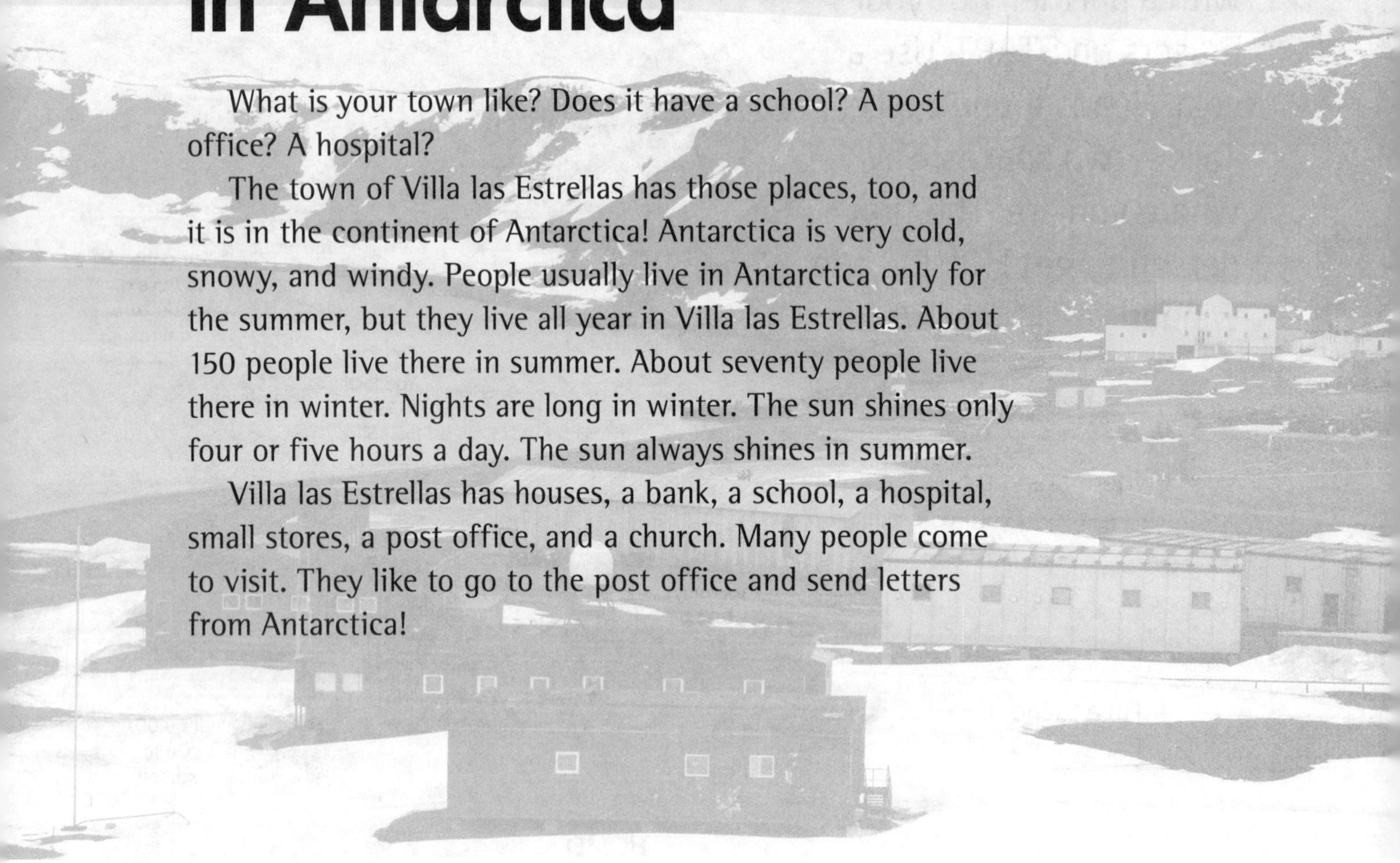

15 **Read.** Check **T** for *True* and **F** for *False*.

1. The night is very long in Antarctica in the summer. Ⓣ Ⓕ
2. Villa las Estrellas has a bank and a school. Ⓣ Ⓕ
3. About 150 people live in Villa las Estrellas in the winter. Ⓣ Ⓕ
4. People like to visit Villa las Estrellas. Ⓣ Ⓕ
5. You can send a letter from Antarctica. Ⓣ Ⓕ

16 Read and match.

1. Where is Villa las Estrellas?
2. What's the weather like in Villa las Estrellas?
3. How long does the sun shine in summer?
4. Can children go to school there?

a. The sun always shines in summer.
b. It's in Antarctica.
c. Yes, they can.
d. It is very cold, snowy, and windy.

17 Complete the chart.

	Villa las Estrellas	Where You Live
Weather		
How many people		
Places		

18 **Check the box.** Take a class survey.

☐ I want to live in Antarctica.

☐ I don't want to live in Antarctica.

How many students want to live in Antarctica?

___

How many students don't want to live in Antarctica?

___

19 Read.

I live in Nagoya, Japan. My favorite place is Nagoya station. It's big. There are two tall towers. You can go to the top of the towers and see the city. There is a gold clock. I meet my friends there, and then we go to the movie theater across the street.

20 Read and write. Read each pair of sentences. Rewrite them as one sentence. Use the word *and* to connect the ideas in the sentences.

1. I go to the park. I play there.

____

2. The park has flowers. It is beautiful.

____

3. The park has trees. It has grass, too.

____

21 Write in your notebook.

1. Where do you live?

2. Where are your two favorite places in your town?

3. What can you do there?

22 Work with a partner. Talk about your favorite places. Find a classmate who has the same favorite place. Talk about it.

23 **Look at the map.** Write directions.

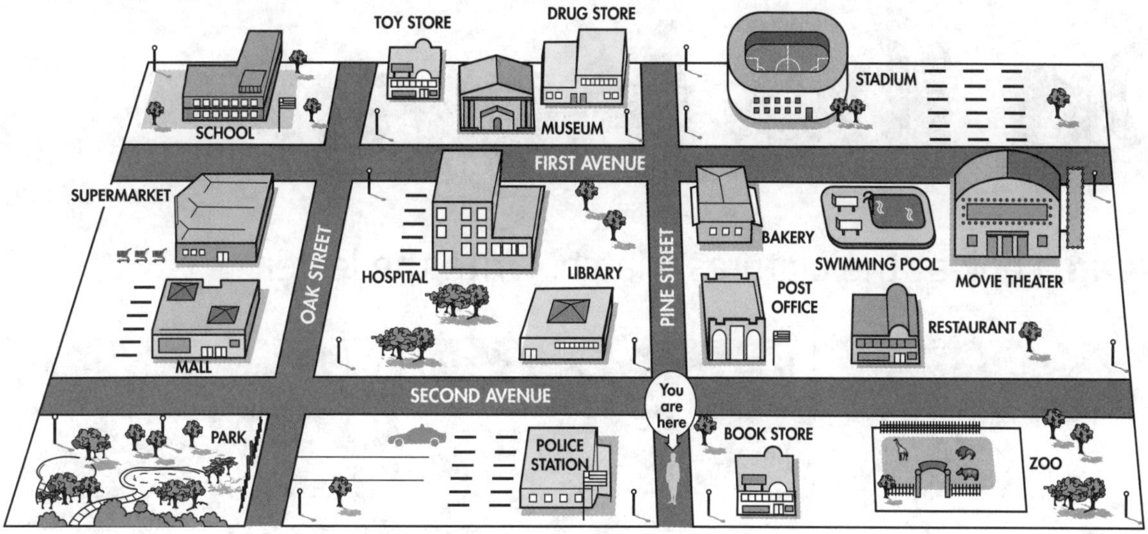

1. How can I get to the bakery?

____

____

2. How can I get to the park?

____

3. How can I get to the museum?

____

____

24 **Look at the map.** Write your own conversation.

How ____?

____

____

Unit 3

On the Move!

1 **Read.** Look at the pictures. Match. Write the letter.

a

b

c

d

e

f

g

h

i

j

k

1. a helicopter ☐
2. a sailboat ☐
3. a hot air balloon ☐
4. a ship ☐
5. a subway ☐
6. a bus ☐
7. an airplane ☐
8. a ferry ☐
9. a scooter ☐
10. a taxi ☐
11. a motorcycle ☐

2 **Read.** Write the words from Activity 1 in the boxes.

It's in the sky.

It's on water.

It's on land.

3 **Listen and check.** Check what the boy and girl like. TR: 17

	ship	subway	airplane	ferry	scooter
boy					
girl					

4 **Listen to the song.** Write. TR: 18

1. I take the ________________ to school.

2. I ride my ________________ to school.

3. I take a ________________ to school. Yes, I do.

4. I take the ________________ to school. Yes, I do.

ferry

bus

subway

bike

5 **Write a new verse for the song.** Use some words from the box.

airplane	helicopter	hot air balloon	taxi	scooter	motorcycle

I fly my ________________ to school. Yes, I do.

I ride my ________________ to school. Do you ride one, too?

I take a ________________ to school. Yes, I do.

I take a ________________ to school. Do you take one, too?

GRAMMAR

I ride my bike to the park.	**I do, too.**	**don't** = do not
I take the bus to the park.	**I don't.** I walk.	
My sister rides her scooter to the park.	My brother **does, too.**	**doesn't** = does not
My big brother rides his motorcycle to the park.	My sister **doesn't.**	

6 Read, look, and match.

1. Rodrigo rides his bike to the bakery.
   His brother does, too.

2. His mother takes a taxi to work.
   His father doesn't.
   He takes a bus.

3. My sister rides her scooter to school. I don't. I walk.

4. My grandfather takes a ferry.
   I do, too.

7 **What about you?** Write a sentence with *do* or *don't*.

1. My friend walks to the museum. I __do, too__.
2. He rides a motorcycle to the post office. I __don't. I take a bus__.
3. He takes the subway to school. I ______________________.
4. He walks to the park. I ______________________.

8 Look, read, and write.

Maya's Family	to school	to work	to the supermarket	to the library
Maya				
Maya's father				
Maya's mother				
Maya's brother				

1. Maya walks to school. Her brother ________________. He takes the subway.
2. Maya's father takes the subway to work. Her mother ________________. She takes a ferry.
3. Maya's brother rides his bike to the library. Maya ________________.
4. Maya's mother takes a bus to the supermarket. Her father ________________.

9 **Write.** Write about how you and someone in your family get around town.

I ________________________ to ________________________.

My ____.

________________________ to ________________________.

10 **Read and write.** Match the sentences to the pictures.

coast downhill   get off   get on   pedal uphill   park

1. Sometimes I help my mother.

   I ______________ my bike,

   and I go to the bakery.

2. The bakery is at the top of a hill.

   I ______________ to the bakery.

3. When I get to the bakery,

   I ______________ my bike.

4. I ______________ my bike

   next to the bakery.

5. After I go to the bakery,

   I ______________ to my home.

a

b

c

d

e

11 **Listen and check.** Check your answers to Activity 10. TR: 19

GRAMMAR

My sister takes a taxi to the mall, **but** my brother rides his bike.

12 **Read and write.** Read the sentences and rewrite using "but."

1. My sister walks to school. My brother rides his bike to school.

   My sister walks to school, but my brother rides his bike to school.

2. I don't like to pedal uphill. I like to coast downhill.

   ____

3. She walks to the movie theater. She takes a bus to the mall.

   ____

4. He eats snacks after school. He always eats his dinner.

   ____

5. A penguin can swim. It can't fly.

   ____

6. The girl is smiling. The boy is frowning.

   ____

7. My mother likes bread. My father likes meat.

   ____

13 **Work with a partner.** Student 1, go to page 122. Student 2, go to page 124. Take turns.

14 **Go through the maze.** Write.

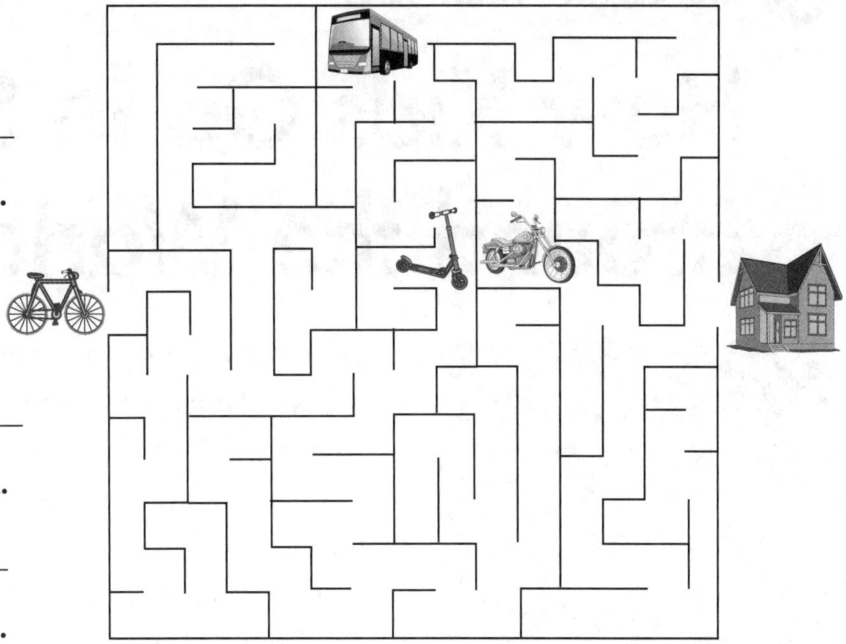

1. I ride a bike to the scooter.
2. I ride the ______ to the ______.
3. I take the ______ to the ______.
4. I ride the ______ to my ______.

15 **Write.** Use words from the box.

scooter	does	taxi	but	doesn't	pedals uphill	coasts downhill

1. Sofia rides her ______ to school. Carlos ______, too.
2. She takes a ______ to the ferry, ______ he rides a motorcycle.
3. Sara ______. Roberto ______. He ______.

16 **Listen and read.** Can you say these fast? TR: 20

1. A motorcycle moves Mary to the mall on Monday.
2. Take a taxi to the tall tower tomorrow.
3. Six scooters scoot to the subway.

17 Listen and read. TR: 21

How Kids Go to School around the World!

How do you get to school? Do you walk? Do you ride your bike? Does your mom or dad drive you to school?

Many children take a school bus to school, but some children in India ride a special school boat! The children live on boats, but they go to school on land. They take the school boat in the morning. A teacher teaches them on the boat before they get to school.

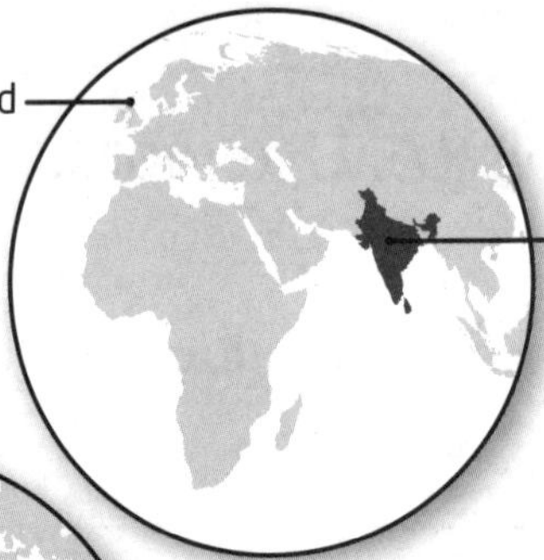

Some children who live in the mountains of Colombia take a zip line to get to school. The zip line is long. The children aren't scared to take the zip line.

One boy in Scotland rides his bike, takes a ferry, and takes a bus to get to school every day. It takes a long time. He gets to school late, but he loves school!

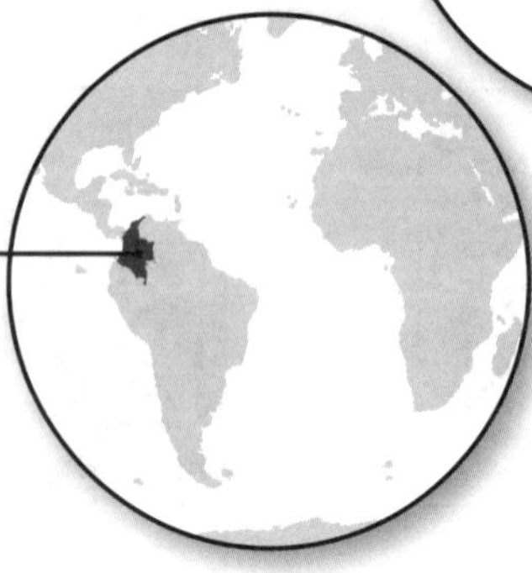

18 Read and write.

school boat   zip line   ferry

1. In Colombia, some children take a ________________ to get to school.
2. One boy in Scotland has to ride his bike, take a ________________, and take a bus to get to school.
3. Some children in India ride a ________________ to school.

19 **Read and write.** Write the sentences in the chart.

Some children who live in the mountains take a zip line.

One boy rides a bike, takes a ferry, and takes a bus.

Some children take a school boat.

How children get to school

- **India**
- **Colombia**
- **Scotland**

20 **Take a survey.** Read and check. Ask and count.

☐ I want to ride a zip line to school.

☐ I want to take a boat to school.

How many students want to ride a zip line to school? ______

How many students want to take a boat to school? ______

weird but true

Fish don't go to school, but a group of fish is called a school!

21 **Read and write.** Read about an amazing bike. Write the paragraph again, using "but" to join the underlined sentences.

My Amazing Bike!

I have an amazing bike. <u>It can fly</u>. <u>It can't swim</u>. Do you have a bike like mine? <u>It can fly to the moon</u>. <u>It can't go under the ocean</u>. <u>I like to ride in the sun</u>. <u>Sometimes I ride in the rain</u>.

____

____

____

____

22 **Write and draw.** Write about your own amazing form of transportation. Use sentences with "but." Draw a picture of it.

My Amazing ______________________

____

____

____

____

____

____

23 Unscramble and write.

1. drives / My / mom / school / to / me

____

2. skateboard / the / to / rides / My / sister / her / park

____

3. doesn't / a bus / school / My / take / brother / to

____

4. How / get to / you / school / do

____

5. pedal / like / I / I / to /to / ride my bike, / like / don't / but / uphill

____

6. on / like to / coast / I / my / bike / downhill

____

7. the subway / school / home / We / after / take

____

8. take / I / a ferry / don't / the stadium / to

____

24 **Write.** Complete the sentences. Write about you.

1. The boy rides a motorcycle, but I ride a bike.
2. The girl wants to fly a helicopter, _______________.
3. She likes to pedal uphill, _______________.
4. He wants to ride a scooter, _______________.

Review

1 Do the crossword puzzle.

Across

1. I take the ___ to school. My sister doesn't. She walks.
3. I play baseball in the ___.
5. The doctors work in a ___.
6. I like to ___ my grandmother.
8. I can watch a soccer game at the ___.
9. I ___ goldfish before school.

Down

1. There is bread at a ___.
2. It's big. It's on the water.
3. A mother elephant can ___ her baby.
4. He takes the ___ to work.
5. I take care of my pet ___.
7. An ___ can fly.

2 Listen. Circle the answers. TR: 22

1. He **makes his bed / feeds his pet** before school.
2. What does he do **before / after** school?
3. He gets on his bike and **coasts downhill / pedals uphill.**
4. I **always / usually** do my homework at four forty-five.

3 **Look at the map.** Read. Write. Use some words from the box to complete the sentences.

across from   Can   get to   Go straight   help   How   left   next to   right

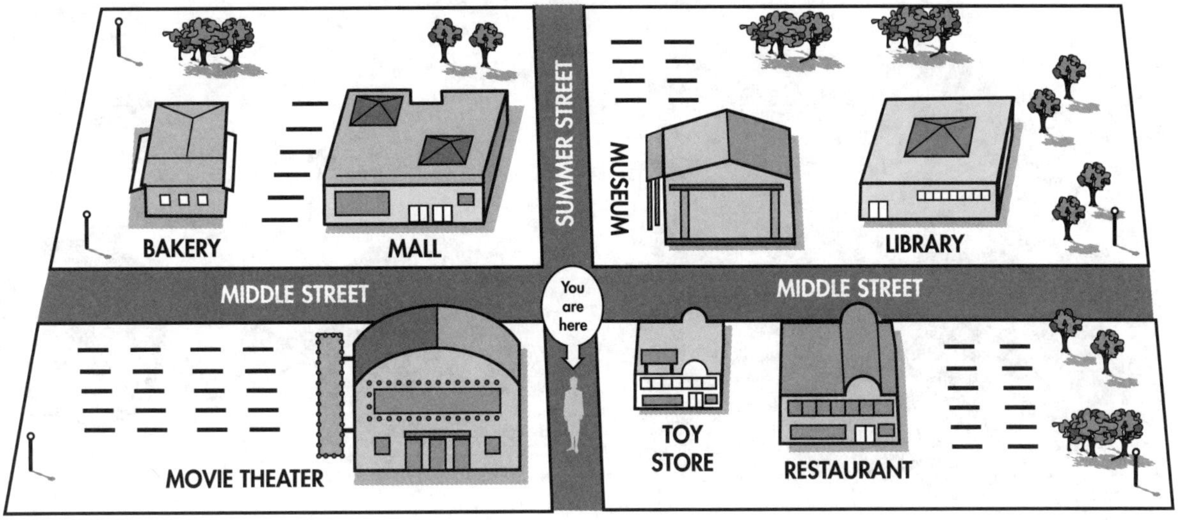

1. ________________ you help me?
2. Sure. How can I ________________?
3. How can I ________________ the bakery?
4. ________________ on Summer Street. Turn ________________ on Middle Street. It's ________________ the mall.

4 **Write.** Use words from the box.

but   do   don't   does   doesn't

1. Ana takes the bus to the mall. Rosa ________________, too.
2. I walk to school, ________________ my sister rides her scooter.
3. Marco takes the subway to the zoo. Maria ________________. She walks.
4. Gracia takes the train to the park. I ________________. I ride my bike.

Unit 4

Our Senses

1 Look at the photos. Circle the hard toys.

2 Listen and write. **TR: 23**

beautiful	delicious	dry	hard	loud	quiet
rough	smooth	soft	sticky	terrible	ugly

1. This hat is ________.
2. This hat is ________.
3. My hands are ________.
4. My hands are ________.
5. This rock is ________.
6. This rock is ________.
7. This apple is ________.
8. This apple is ________.

3 **Look at the pictures.** Read the sentences in Activity 2. Match. Write the number.

a

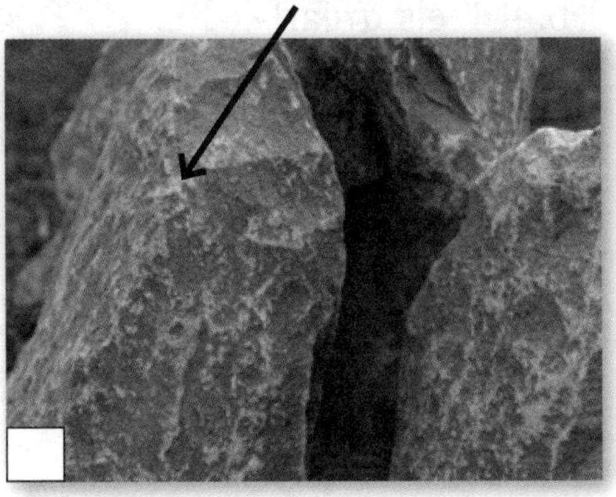

b

c

d

e

f

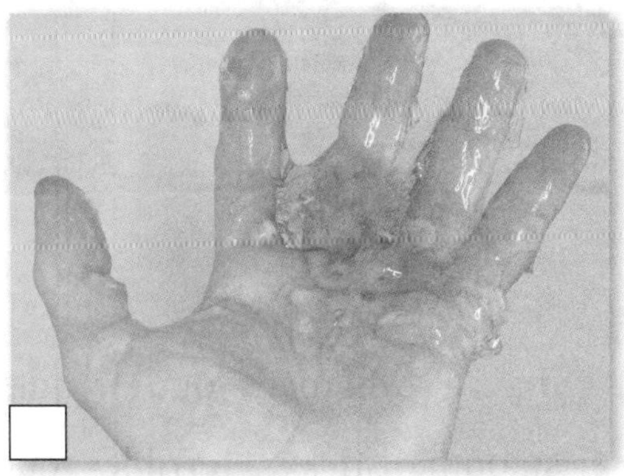

g

h

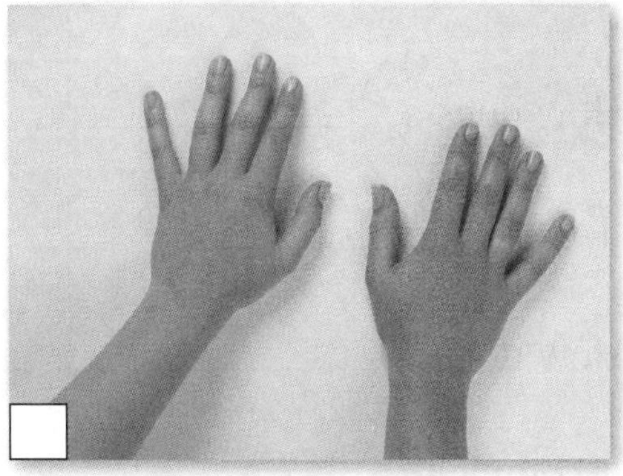

4 **Listen to the song.** Draw lines to match. TR: 24

1. How does the cake taste?
2. How does a kitten feel?
3. How does the garden look?
4. How does a hug feel?
5. How does the drum sound?
6. How does a flower smell?

a. It smells good.
b. It feels great!
c. It feels soft.
d. It tastes sweet.
e. It looks beautiful.
f. It sounds loud.

5 **Write a new verse for the song!** Use some of the images and words from the box.

a banana

a rabbit

a turtle

a hot air balloon

a motorcycle

a subway

dry	hard	loud	quiet
smooth	sticky	terrible	rough

How does a ____________________ feel?

It feels ____________________.

How does a ____________________ sound?

It sounds ____________________.

GRAMMAR

The cheese pizza **smells** great.
The dress **looks** beautiful.
How **does** the apple **taste**?
How **do** the grapes **feel**?

The helicopter **sounds** loud.
The cat **feels** soft.
It **tastes** delicious.
They **feel** smooth.

6 **Look.** Read and match. Write the letter.

a

b
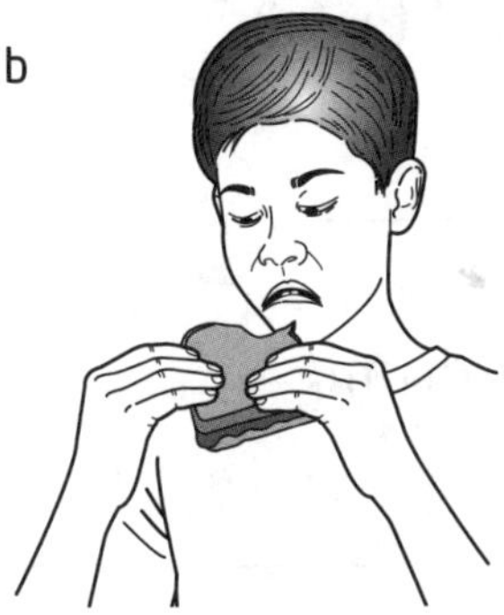

c
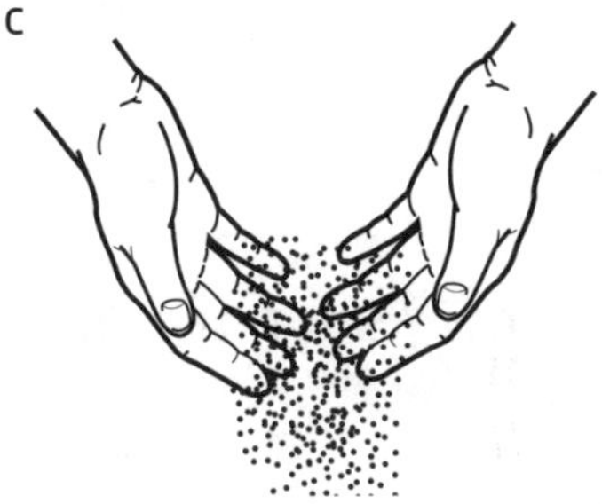

d

e

f

1. This looks beautiful. ____
2. This smells terrible. ____
3. This feels sticky. ____
4. This feels dry. ____
5. This tastes terrible. ____
6. This tastes delicious. ____

7 **Unscramble the sentences.** Write. Listen to check your answers. **TR: 25**

1. feels / The / hot. / sun

____

2. old. / look / books / The

____

3. sandwiches / do / How / the / taste?

____

4. How / sound? / does / the / drum/

____

8 **Read and write.**

1. How does the bread taste? It __________ good.
2. How __________ the sock smell? It smells terrible!
3. How do the rocks feel? They __________ hard.
4. How __________ the old cars look? They look ugly.
5. How __________ the parrot sound? It sounds loud.

9 **Look.** Write about the food. Use words from the box.

look
smell
taste

____

____

____

10 **Read and write.** Listen and check. TR: 26

bitter salty sour spicy sweet

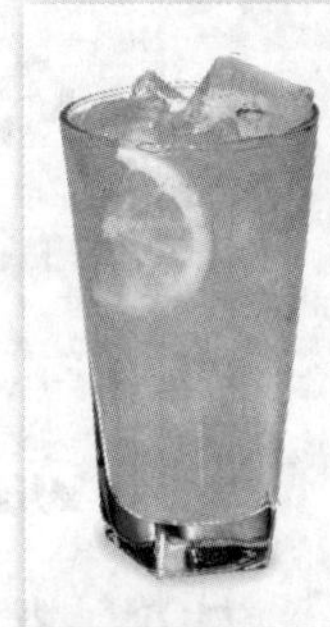

1. My mother drinks tea every morning,

   but I don't like it. It's ______.

2. Lemons are sour, but sometimes lemonade is ______.
3. There are peppers in the soup. It's very ______.
4. This cheese pizza is very ______.
5. This apple isn't sweet. It's ______.

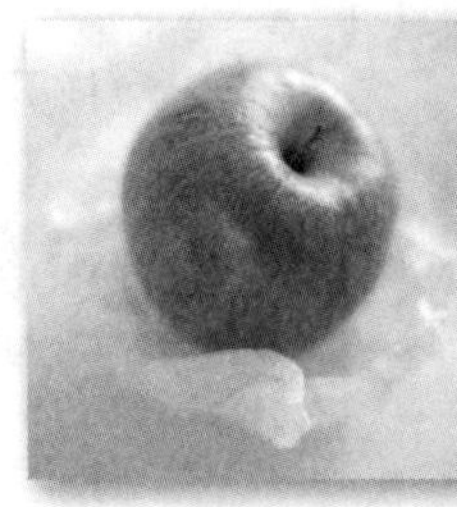

11 **Read and write.** Sort the words. Work with a partner.

apples bananas cheese chips cookies mangoes
nuts oranges salad soup peppers tea yogurt

Apples are sweet.

Sometimes apples are sour.

sweet	sour	salty	spicy	bitter
apples	apples			

GRAMMAR

How **is** the bread?	It'**s** good.	It's = It is
How **are** the grapes?	They **are** good.	
How **was** the bread?	It **was** good. More please!	
How **were** the grapes?	They **were** good. Can I have one more, please?	

12 **Read.** Look and match. Draw lines.

1. The bread is good.
2. The grapes are good.
3. The bread was good.
4. The grapes were good.

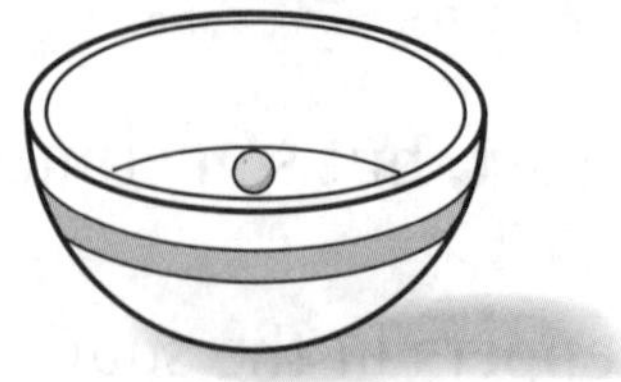

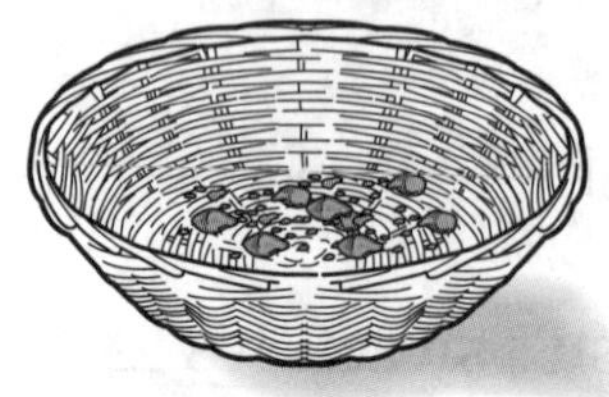

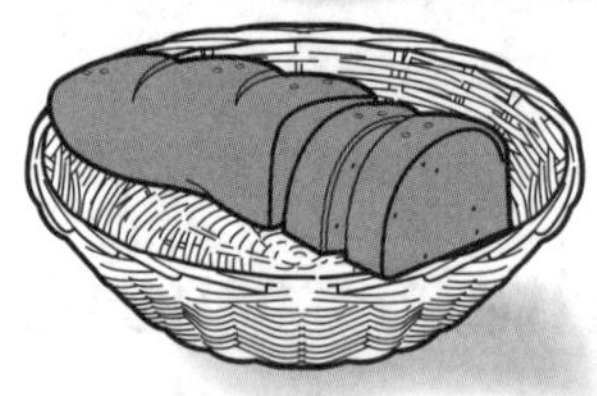

13 **Read and write.**

1. That chair ______ soft, but this chair is hard.
2. How ______ the noodles? They were salty.
3. The baby ______ quiet, but now he is crying.
4. How are your hands? They ______ sticky.
5. That rock was rough, but this rock ______ smooth.
6. How were the tomatoes? They ______ sweet.

14 **Work with a partner.** Student 1, go to page 119. Student 2, go to page 121. Take turns.

15 Do the crossword puzzle.

Across

1. It's in my classroom. It's white. It feels sticky.
5. It's red. It's delicious. Sometimes it's in a salad.
6. Sometimes it's green. Sometimes it's red. It's spicy.
8. It's tall. It's brown and rough. It has green leaves.
9. It can be hard or soft. It's sweet. It tastes delicious.

Down

2. It's yellow. It's sour.
3. It looks beautiful. It smells good.
4. It's small. It feels soft. It has long ears.
7. It's in my classroom. It's smooth.

16 **Look.** Imagine you are in the pictures. Write.

1. How ______________ your hands?
   They ____________________.
2. How ______________ the soccer game?
   It ____________________________.

17 **Listen and read.** Can you say these fast? TR: 27

1. I eat sweet and sour ice cream on Sunday.
2. Billions of bitter beans bounced on the bed.
3. Taste the terrible tea tomorrow.

18 Listen and read. TR: 28

Stinky Animals and Plants

a rafflesia flower

Many things smell good. Apple trees, flowers, and the ocean all smell great. But some animals and plants smell terrible!

The Eastern snake-necked turtle lives in freshwater in eastern Australia. This turtle has a really long neck that looks like a snake. If you catch an Eastern snake-necked turtle, it smells terrible. Some people think it smells like a skunk. In Australia, people call this turtle the "stinker"!

Many flowers smell good, but the rafflesia doesn't. It smells terrible! The rafflesia is the biggest flower in the world. It's almost one meter (three feet) wide. The rafflesia grows in southeastern Asia. The rafflesia smells like old meat. Flies like the smell, and they fly to the rafflesia flower.

an Eastern snake-necked turtle

a skunk

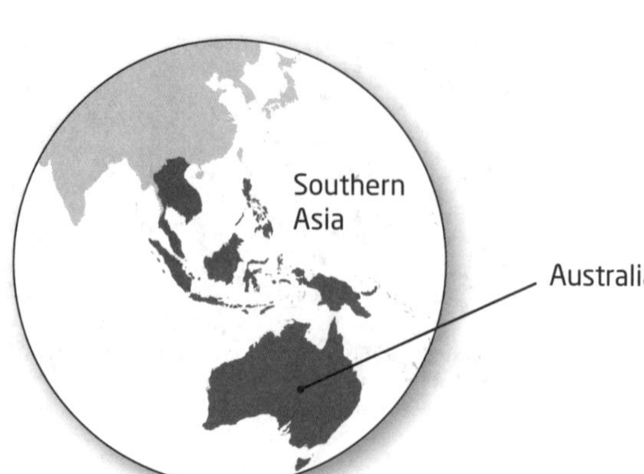

skunk cabbage

Weird but true: **The skunk cabbage is a plant. It smells like a skunk.**

19 **Read.** Check **T** for *True* and **F** for *False*.

1. The rafflesia smells terrible. Ⓣ Ⓕ
2. The Eastern snake-necked turtle has a short neck. Ⓣ Ⓕ
3. Flies like the smell of the rafflesia. Ⓣ Ⓕ
4. The Eastern snake-necked turtle always smells bad. Ⓣ Ⓕ
5. The rafflesia is a very big flower. Ⓣ Ⓕ

20 **Read.** Complete the chart.

Stinky animals and plants

animal: Eastern snake-necked turtle

Where does it live? *It lives in freshwater in eastern Australia.*

What does it smell like? ______

When does it smell terrible? *It smells terrible when you catch it.*

plant: rafflesia

Where does it grow? *It grows in southeastern Asia.*

What does it smell like? ______

What likes its smell? ______

21 **Work with a partner.** Ask and answer. Check and write. Do you want to have an Eastern snake-necked turtle at home?

	Yes	No	Why?
you			
your partner			

22 **Read and write.** Read about winter. Use *or* to join the underlined sentences. Write the sentences.

I like winter. We throw snowballs. Sometimes we build a snowman. We feel cold after we play in the snow. We sit by the fireplace. Sometimes we take a hot shower. Then we have a snack. We eat soup. Sometimes we drink hot chocolate.

____

____

____

23 **Write and draw.** What do you do during school vacation? Write. Use sentences with *or* to show choices. Draw a picture.

____

____

____

24 **Read and choose.** Write the best answer.

1. I don't like this tea. It ________ bitter.
   a. smells b. tastes c. looks
2. The children were listening to the teacher. They were ________.
   a. quiet b. dry c. loud
3. How was the mango? It ________ delicious!
   a. is b. was c. were
4. I like this sweater. It ________ soft.
   a. sounds b. smells c. feels
5. A lemon is ________.
   a. sour b. sweet c. spicy
6. How ________ the potato chips? They were great! More please!
   a. is b. was c. were

25 **Read and write.** Use words from the box.

terrible loud spicy salty sweet soft sticky quiet hard

1. How was the music? The music was loud.
2. How were the noodles? ____________________
3. How was the restaurant? ____________________
4. How were the beans? ____________________

26 **Work with a partner.** Read. Describe. Write.

	yogurt	nuts	crocodile	ocean
look	white			
sound				
taste	sweet, sour			
feel	smooth			
smell	delicious			

Unit 5

Animal Habitats

1 **Look and match.** Write the number.

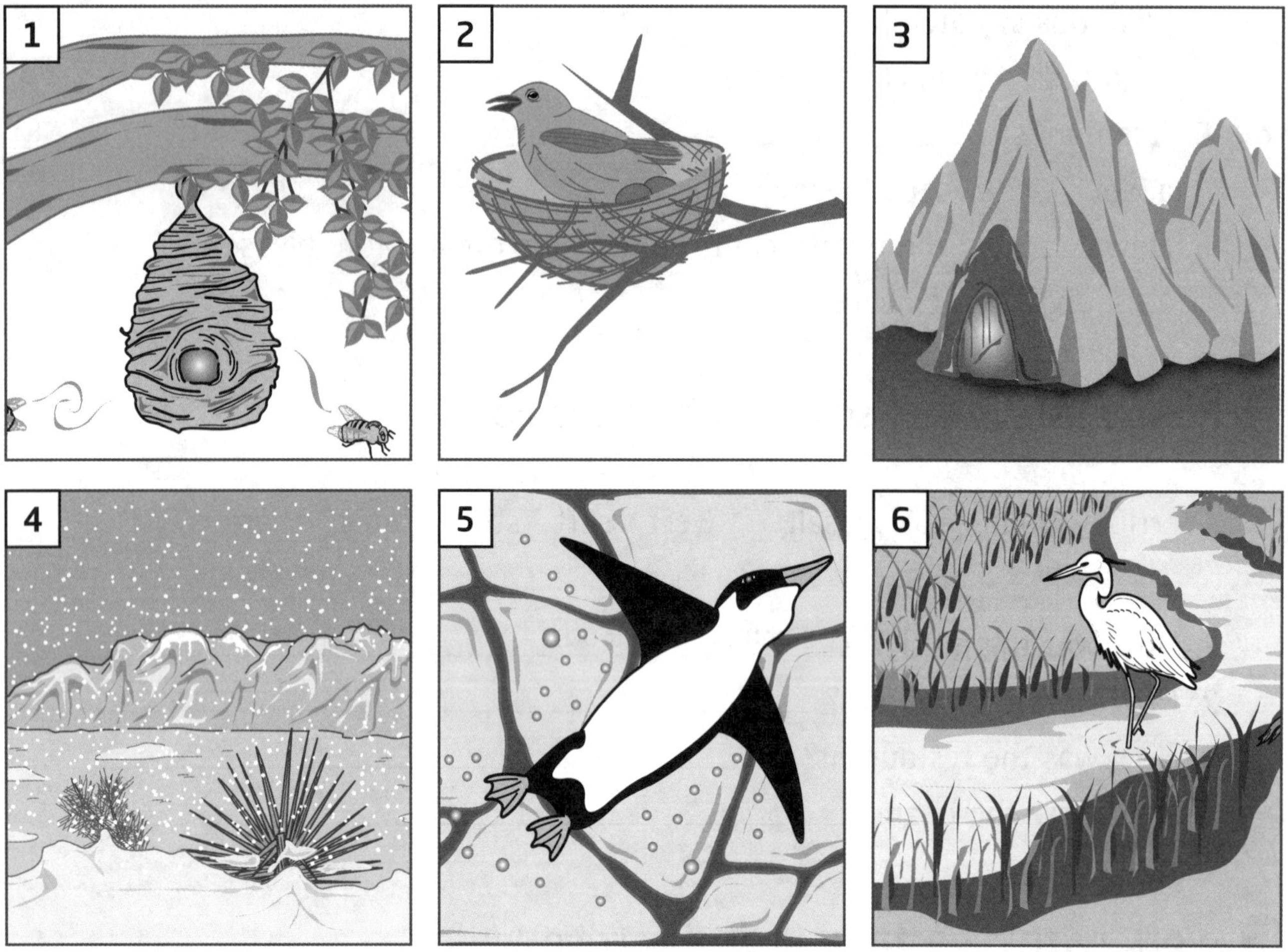

☐ grasslands	☐ a web	☐ ice	☐ a forest	☐ a desert
☐ an island	☐ underground	☐ wetlands	☐ a nest	☐ mud
☐ a hive	☐ snow	☐ a rain forest	☐ a cave	

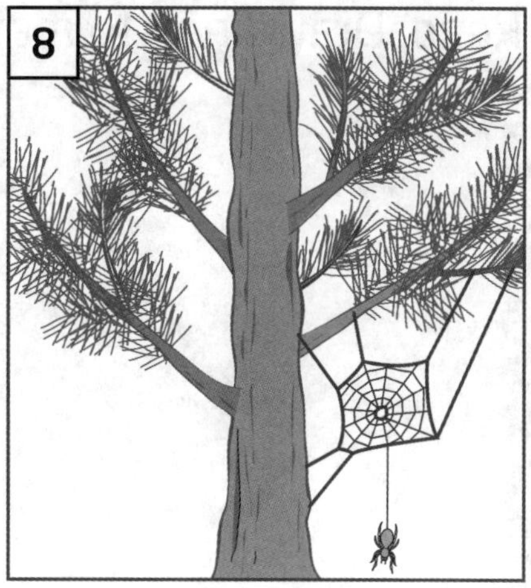

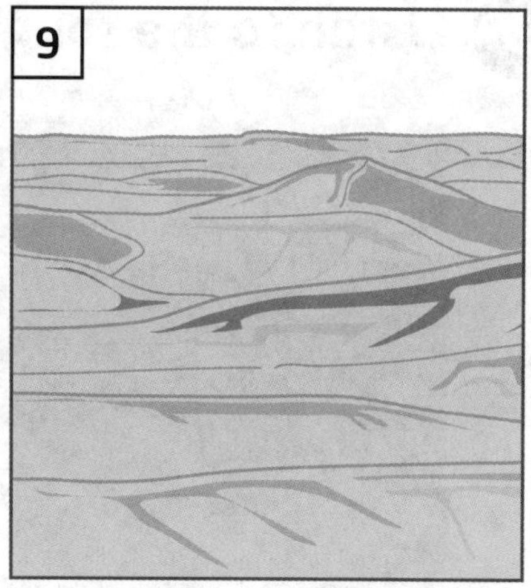

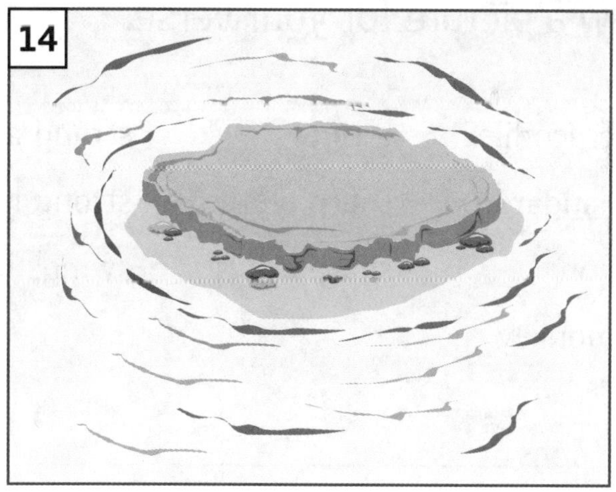

2 **Look at the pictures.** Read and write.

1. What's the turtle crawling in? ________________
2. What's above the penguin? ________________
3. Where do trees grow? ______________________________________

3 **Listen to the song.** Read. Draw lines to match. **TR: 29**

1. Why does a giraffe have a long, long neck?
2. Why does a frog have strong legs?
3. Why does a polar bear have white fur?

a. Because it lives in ice and snow.
b. Because it eats leaves at the tops of the trees.
c. Because it hops, swims, and jumps.

4 **Write a new verse for the song!** Use some words from the box. Draw a picture for your verse.

a crocodile	a tiger	strong arms	eats meat
a kangaroo	sharp teeth	strong legs	hops
a lion	sharp claws	swings in trees	climbs trees
a monkey			

Why does ______________________ have ______________________?

Why? Why?

Because it ______________

____

______________________.

GRAMMAR

Why does a horse run fast? **Because** it has strong legs.
Why is the bear in the cave? **Because** the bear lives in the cave.
Why can frogs jump and hop? **Because** they have strong legs.
Why don't you like crocodiles? **Because** they are scary.
Why can't ducks climb trees? **Because** ducks don't have arms.

5 **Read and write.** Use words from the box.

are Because do does don't is Why

1. Why don't fish run?
Because they don't have legs.

2. _________ hippos stand in water?
_________ the sun is hot, and hippos feel cool in the water.

3. _________ the parrot eating a nut?
_________ parrots like nuts.

4. _________ the desert dry?
_________ there is very little rain in the desert.

5. _________ the birds in the wetlands?
_________ they eat frogs and fish, and frogs and fish live in the wetlands.

6. _________ the tiger drink water?
_________ it is thirsty.

7. _________ zebras live underground?
_________ zebras eat grass, and there isn't any grass underground.

6 **Read and match.** Draw lines.

1. Why is the rabbit going underground?
2. Why don't penguins live on grasslands?
3. Why are the zebras running?
4. Why are the elephants in the water?
5. Why is the bird flying to the nest?

a. Because they are taking a bath.
b. Because its home is underground.
c. Because penguins need to eat fish and food in the ocean.
d. Because its babies are in the nest.
e. Because they see a lion, and they are scared.

7 **Write sentences.** Work with a partner. Read your partner's sentences. Ask your partner questions. Use words from the box.

caves	forests
webs	hives
ice	islands
mud	rain forests
snow	grasslands

I like rain forests.

Why do you like rain forests?

Because I like monkeys and parrots, and they live in rain forests.

I like ______________________.

I don't like ______________________.

8 **Listen and write.** Use words from the box. TR: 30

fur horns pouch tongue wings

1. A kangaroo has a __________.
2. A butterfly has __________. It can fly.
3. A frog has a long, sticky __________.
4. A goat has two __________ on its head.
5. A lion has __________.

9 **Look and read.** Check **T** for *True* and **F** for *False*.

1. A giraffe has a long tongue. (T) (F)
2. A cow has a pouch. (T) (F)
3. A chicken has wings. (T) (F)
4. A panda has black and white fur. (T) (F)
5. A donkey has horns. (T) (F)

GRAMMAR

Kangaroos use their pouches **to carry** their babies.

Parrots use their wings **to fly**.

Cats use their tongues **to clean** their fur.

10 Listen and write. TR: 31

to carry	to clean	to eat	to fight	to fly
to jump	to protect	to run	to swim	to hide

1. Goats use their horns ________________.
2. Polar bears use their white fur ________________ in the ice and snow.
3. Lions use their teeth ________________ meat.
4. Horses use their legs ________________.
5. Ostriches use their legs ________________ fast.
6. Giraffes use their long tongues ________________ their eyes.
7. Tigers use their mouths ________________ their babies.
8. Penguins use their wings ________________.
9. Cats use their sharp claws ________________ their babies.
10. Owls use their wings ________________.

11 What about you? What do you use? Write.

1. What do you use to eat? ________________________________
2. What do you use to walk? ________________________________
3. What do you use to write? ________________________________

12 Work with a partner. Student 1, go to page 123. Student 2, go to page 125. Take turns.

13 **Read the clues.** Do the puzzle.

1. Why can a frog catch a fly with its ______? Because it is sticky.
2. Why can't a zebra fly? Because it doesn't have ______.
3. Goats use their ______ to fight.
4. Why does an owl have big eyes? ______ it needs to see at night.
5. Many turtles live in ______.
6. Lions live in ______.
7. Camels live in the ______.
8. Big spiders live in the ______.

1. GEONUT _ _ _ _ _ _ (2, 14)
2. GIWSN _ _ _ _ _ (3)
3. HONRS _ _ _ _ _ (13)
4. CEABESU _ _ _ _ _ _ _ (7, 6, 9)
5. LATDENSW _ _ _ _ _ _ _ _ (5, 10)
6. GAASLRDNSS _ _ _ _ _ _ _ _ _ _ (4, 11)
7. RETSED _ _ _ _ _ _ (8)
8. IRNA SROFTE _ _ _ _ ■ _ _ _ _ _ _ (1, 12)

_ _ _ M _ _ _   _ _ _   _ M _ Z _ _ _ !

1 2 3 4 5 6   7 8 9   10 11 12 13 14

14 **Listen and read.** Can you say these fast? **TR: 32**

1. My nephew never stands next to a nest.
2. We walk through the wetlands in windy weather.
3. Do the polar bear and panda play in the park?

15 Listen and read. TR: 33

The Coolest Animals Live in Antarctica!

Antarctica is very cold, very dry, and very windy. Can animals live there? Yes, they can!

The emperor penguin is a bird. It can't fly, but it can swim. The mother penguin lays an egg on the ice. Where is the nest for this egg? The father emperor penguin takes care of the egg. He puts it on his feet! Why? Because he can keep the egg warm.

The Weddell seal lives in Antarctica, too. It spends a lot of time in the ocean. It can stay under water for forty-five minutes. The seal swims under the ice. Why? Because it catches fish and eats under water. It is safe under the ice.

The Arctic tern is a small but amazing bird. It lives in Antarctica in the winter and flies to the Arctic in the summer! Why do the terns fly to the Arctic? Because the birds make nests there. The nests are on the ground. The mother lays eggs in the nest. The parents protect their nest and their babies. The parents feed the young birds, too.

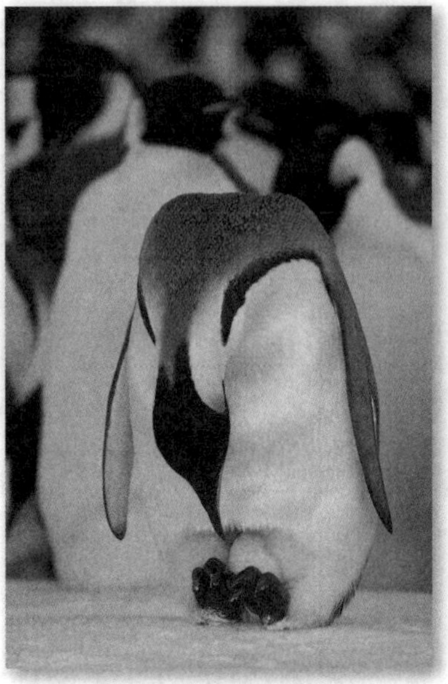

emperor penguin

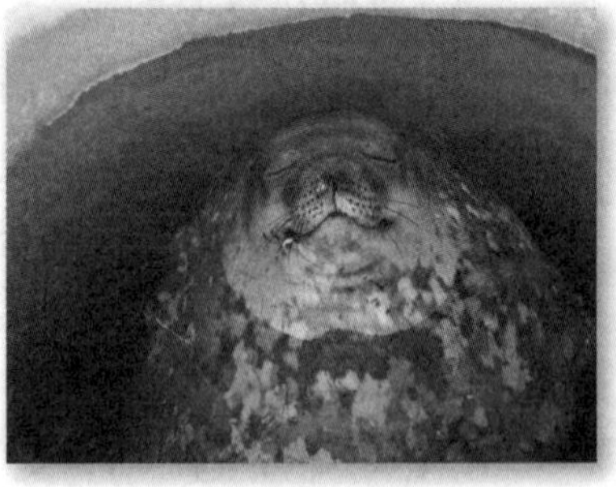

Weddell seal

Arctic tern

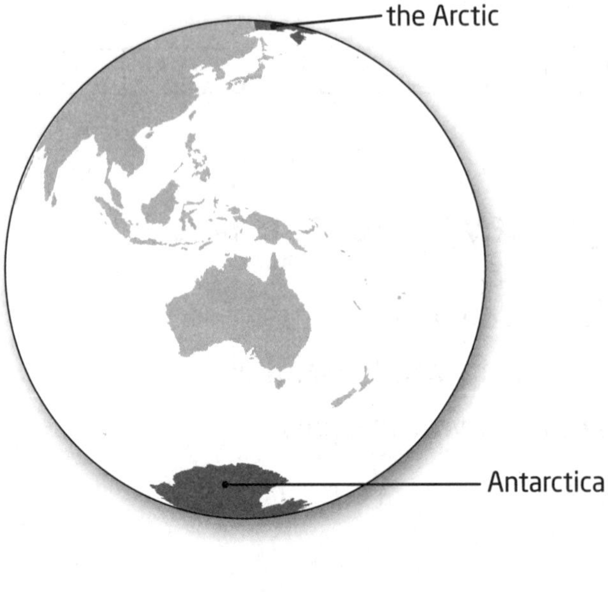

16 **Read.** Check **T** for *True* and **F** for *False*.

1. The emperor penguin can swim well. (T) (F)
2. The emperor penguin father takes care of the egg. (T) (F)
3. The Weddell seal can swim under the ice. (T) (F)
4. Antarctica is hot and sunny. (T) (F)
5. The Arctic tern flies to the Arctic in the summer. (T) (F)

17 **Complete the chart.** Work with a partner. Talk about animals of Antarctica.

Animal	What can it do?	More information
emperor penguin	The __________ lays an egg on the ice. The father takes care of the egg.	The __________ puts the egg on his feet. He keeps the egg warm.
__________	It spends a lot of time in the ocean.	It can swim under the ice. It eats __________.
Arctic tern	It flies between __________ __________.	It lives __________ in the winter. It flies to the Arctic in the summer. It builds a nest and lays eggs in the Arctic.

18 **Read and write.**

1. The father emperor penguin takes care of the __________.
2. The Weddell seal can swim under the __________.
3. The Arctic tern flies between __________ and the Arctic.
4. The Arctic tern builds a __________ in the Arctic.

weird but true

Polar bears live in the Arctic. A polar bear's fur is white, but its skin is black!

19 **Read.** Underline the words that tell what the animal looks like and what the animal does. Write the name of the animal.

It lives in grasslands. It is brown and yellow. It can run. It has long legs and a long neck. It eats leaves at the tops of trees. It uses its long tongue to clean its eyes and ears.

What is it?

It's a ______________.

20 **Draw a picture of an animal.** Describe it. Tell where it lives. Tell what it looks like. Tell what it does.

This animal lives ____________________. It is ____________________.

It can ____________________. It has ____________________.

It eats ______________. It uses its ______________ to ______________.

21 **Work with a partner.** Read your description from Activity 20 to a partner. Ask, "What is the animal?" Write the answer.

What is the animal? It's ______________.

22 **Look at the picture.** Circle the hive, the cave, the web, the mud, and the nest.

23 **Look at the picture in Activity 22.** Read and write. Use some words from the box.

a forest	Because	fur	grasslands	wetlands	nest
snow	to eat	to hop	to see	Why	wings

1. The animals live in ________________.
2. A butterfly uses its ________________ to fly.
3. The rabbit has soft ________________.
4. The rabbit uses its legs ________________.
5. The turtle uses its eyes ________________.
6. ________________ is one bear big? Because it's the mother.
7. Why is one bear small? ________________ it's a baby bear.
8. The bird is in the ________________.

Unit 6

What's for Dinner?

1 Listen and write. TR: 34

a piece	a can	a jar	a loaf	a glass
a bunch	a bag	a bowl	a box	a bottle

1. __________ of rice ☐
2. __________ of cake ☐
3. __________ of sugar ☐
4. __________ of oil ☐
5. __________ of olives ☐
6. __________ of soda ☐
7. __________ of bananas ☐
8. __________ of juice ☐
9. __________ of cereal ☐
10. __________ of bread ☐

a

b

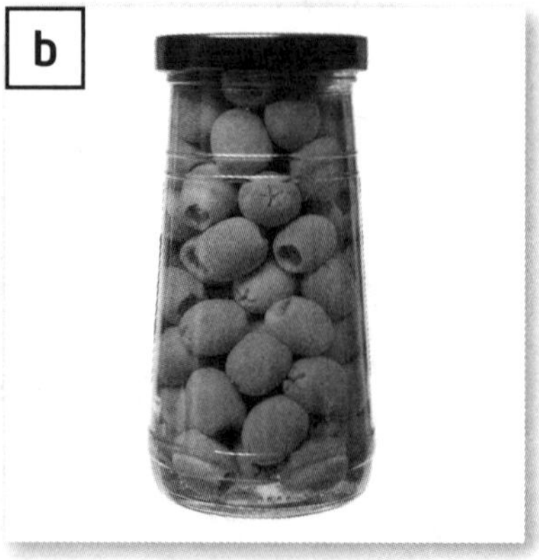

2 **Read the words in Activity 1.** Look at the pictures. Match.
Write the letters in the boxes next to the words.

c

d

e

f

g

h

i

j

3 **Listen to the song.** Look at the pictures. Read. Check ✓ the box when you hear the word. **TR: 35**

☐ a bowl of rice

☐ a bowl of ice cream

☐ a bowl of pasta

☐ a can of soda

☐ a glass of milk

☐ bread

☐ a cake

☐ a cookie

4 **Listen and write.** **TR: 36**

1. A jar of jelly is no fun,
   if there isn't any ________________ to spread it on.
   ________________ is very nice,
   but it tastes better with some spice.
2. ________________, a jar of spice,
   ________________, and ________________ are nice!
   Let's go now. Let's buy some food.
   Let's go shopping, just me and you!

GRAMMAR

Are there **any** boxes of cereal?	Yes, there are **some** on the table.
Are there **any** loaves of bread?	No, there aren't **any**.
Is there **any** cheese?	Yes, there is **some** in the fridge.
Is there **any** rice?	No, there isn't **any**.

5 **Listen.** Read and circle. **TR: 37**

1. Is there any cake?
   Yes, there is some.   No, there isn't any.
2. Are there any bottles of oil?
   Yes, there are some.   No, there aren't any.
3. Are there any pieces of cake?
   Yes, there are some.   No, there aren't any.
4. Is there any cereal?
   Yes, there is some.   No, there isn't any.

6 **Look at the picture.** Read and write.

1. Are there ___any___ beans?
   Yes, there are some in a jar.
2. Are there ________ cans of soda?
   ____
3. Is there ________ orange juice?
   ____
4. Are there ________ eggs?
   ____
5. Are there ________ bottles of apple juice?
   ____

7 **Circle five foods.** Draw them. Look at your picture. Answer the questions. Use *any* or *some* in your answers.

bags of rice	bags of sugar	bottles of oil
bottles of milk	boxes of cereal	boxes of noodles
bunches of bananas	bunches of grapes	cans of soda
jars of olives	loaves of bread	pieces of cake

1. Are there any bunches of bananas? ____________
2. Is there any bread? ____________
3. Are there any olives? ____________
4. Is there any oil? ____________
5. Are there any boxes of noodles? ____________

8 **Work with a partner.** Don't show your picture from Activity 7. Have your partner ask questions about your picture. Answer.

Are there any bags of sugar?

No, there aren't any.

Is there any cereal?

Yes, there is some.

9 **Listen and read.** Write. TR: 38

1. The __________ of that hamburger is seventy-five cents.
2. Let's __________ the milk and eggs in the refrigerator.
3. I'm hungry. Let's go to the supermarket and __________ some food.
4. Which is better, yogurt or ice cream? Let's __________ them.
5. Oh no! I don't have any __________! I can't take the bus home.

10 **Read and write.** Use words from the box. Use some words more than one time.

buy	compare	money	price	put away

1. I'm thirsty. Let's __________ a can of soda.
2. The __________ of that bag of nuts is fifty cents.
3. I have twenty cents. Do you have any __________?
4. Yes, I have some __________.
5. I have ninety cents. We can __________ a bag of nuts and a can of soda.
6. Which snack is better for me? I need to __________ them.
7. I __________ my toys after I play.

GRAMMAR

Are there any nuts?	Yes, there are **a few**.
Are there any olives in the salad?	Yes, there are **a few**.
Are there any apples?	Yes, there are **a few** in the bag.
Is there any tea?	Yes, there is **a little**.
Is there any juice?	Yes, there is **a little** in the bottle.

11 **Read.** Write the foods in the correct columns in the chart.

bunches of bananas, hamburgers, ice cream, milk, soup, loaves of bread, potatoes, salad, sandwiches

There are a few.	There is a little.
bunches of bananas	*milk*

12 **Read and write.** Use *is a little* or *are a few.*

1. Are there any bags of rice? Yes, there ________________.
2. Are there any boxes of cereal? Yes, there ________________.
3. Is there any oil in the bottle? Yes, there ________________.
4. Is there any pasta in the bowl? Yes, there ________________.
5. Are there any cans of soda? Yes, there ________________.
6. Is there any sugar in the bowl? Yes, there ________________.
7. Is there any cake? Yes, there ________________.

13 **Work with a partner.** Student 1, go to page 118. Student 2, go to page 126. Take turns.

14 **Work with a partner.** What's in your classroom? Answer the questions. Write. Use sentences from the box.

Yes, there is some.	Yes, there are a few.	Yes, there is a little.
Yes, there are some.	No, there isn't any.	No, there aren't any.

1. Is there any water? ______
2. Are there any bags? ______
3. Is there any soda? ______
4. Is there any glue? ______
5. Are there any snacks? ______
6. Are there any windows? ______

15 **Look at the pictures.** Circle the words.

h	k	d	p	r	i	c	e
c	s	x	y	q	g	p	a
m	o	z	c	w	t	p	j
q	a	m	z	x	s	w	b
e	f	v	p	b	g	t	u
p	u	t	★	a	w	a	y
y	j	m	i	k	r	l	u
o	p	l	m	o	n	e	y

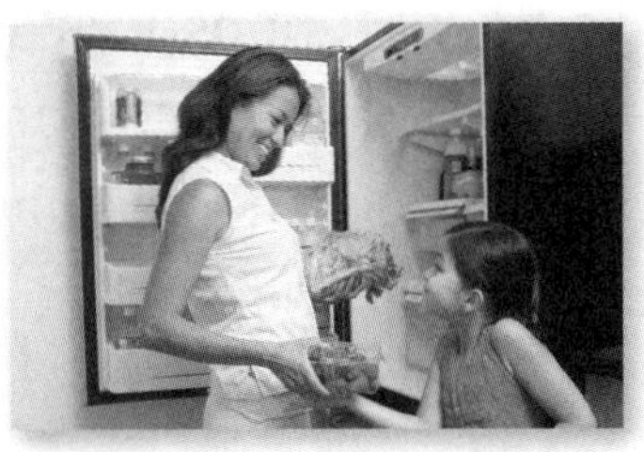

16 **Listen and read.** Can you say these fast? **TR: 39**

1. Put away the pasta, peppers, and potatoes.
2. Betty buys a big bunch of bananas.
3. Compare the cheese, chips, and chicken carefully.

17 **Listen and read.** TR: 40

How People Eat

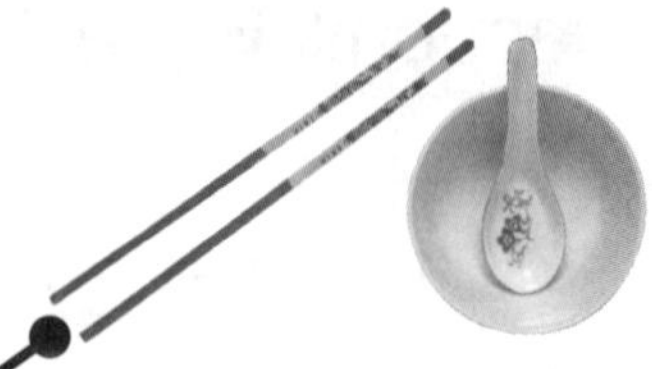

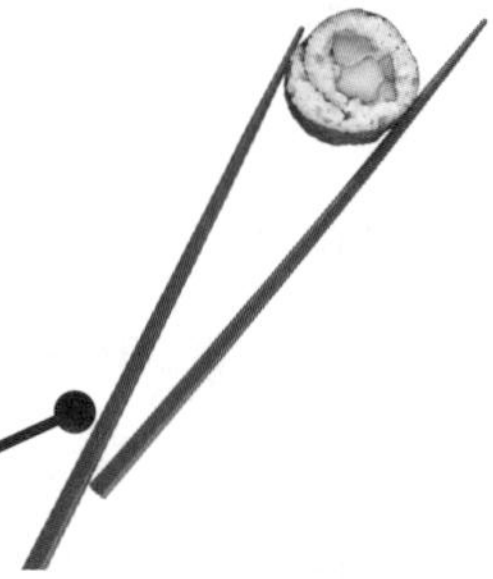

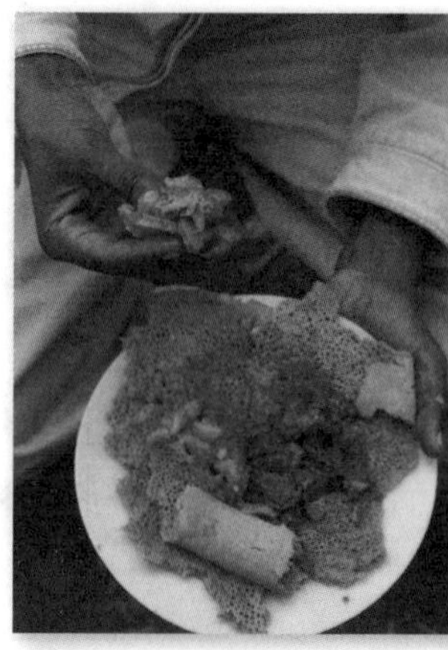

People eat in different ways. People in China, Japan, and Korea usually use chopsticks to eat. Chopsticks are different in each country. Chopsticks in China are long, and they are round at the end. Chopsticks in Japan are pointed at the end, and chopsticks in Korea are made of metal.

People use chopsticks in Thailand and Cambodia, but they only use chopsticks to eat noodles. They use a spoon and fork to eat other foods.

People in Europe and the Americas usually use forks, knives, and spoons to eat. But people in India and Ethiopia use bread to pick up food. They eat with their right hand. People in many places use their hands to eat hamburgers and pizza.
What do you use to eat?

18 **Read.** Check **T** for *True* and **F** for *False*.

1. All chopsticks look the same. Ⓣ Ⓕ
2. People in India eat with their right hand. Ⓣ Ⓕ
3. People in Cambodia always use chopsticks. Ⓣ Ⓕ
4. People in Europe usually use forks, knives, and spoons. Ⓣ Ⓕ

19 **Read and check.** What do people usually use to eat?

	chopsticks	knives	forks	spoons	bread
China	✓				
Japan					
Korea					
Thailand					
Cambodia					
Europe and the Americas					
India and Ethiopia					

20 **Work with a partner.** What do you use to eat? Complete the chart. Check.

	chopsticks	knives	forks	spoons	bread	hands
You						
Your partner						

weird but true

A chimpanzee uses a stick to eat ants.

21 **Read.** Answer the questions. Write.

My Favorite Birthday Food

Tacos are my favorite birthday food. I love corn tacos filled with spicy meat, fish, or chicken. I like tomatoes and vegetables in my tacos. I eat tacos with my hands! Tacos are fun to eat. They taste delicious, too!

1. Underline the topic sentence of the paragraph.
2. Do the other sentences give more information about the topic, or main idea? ______

22 **Write and draw.** What is your favorite birthday food? Write about it. First write a sentence to tell the topic, or main idea. Write other sentences to tell more about your favorite birthday food. Draw a picture of your favorite birthday food.

____

____

____

____

23 **Look at the photos.** Write questions and answers. Use words from the box.

Are there any	Yes, there are some. Yes, there are a few. No, there aren't any.
Is there any	Yes, there is some. Yes, there is a little. No, there isn't any.

1. ______________ bottles of oil? ______________
2. ______________ milk? ______________
3. ______________ sugar? ______________
4. ______________ boxes of cereal? ______________
5. ______________ glasses of juice? ______________

24 **What about you?** Read and write.

1. Where do you use money? ______________
2. What do you like to buy? ______________
3. What do you compare? ______________
4. Do you put away your clothes and toys? ______________

Review

1 **Look at the photos.** Circle the words in the puzzle.

d	p	o	f	o	r	e	s	t
u	e	y	t	r	w	q	l	k
b	h	l	g	f	d	s	a	m
u	b	v	i	s	l	a	n	d
n	s	t	i	c	k	y	x	z
c	r	w	s	h	i	v	e	x
h	f	v	c	t	s	o	f	t
b	h	y	j	k	v	l	u	f
q	x	w	r	g	l	a	s	s

2 **Look.** Read and match. Write the letter.

a

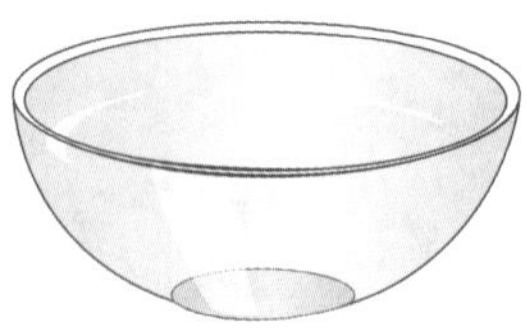
b

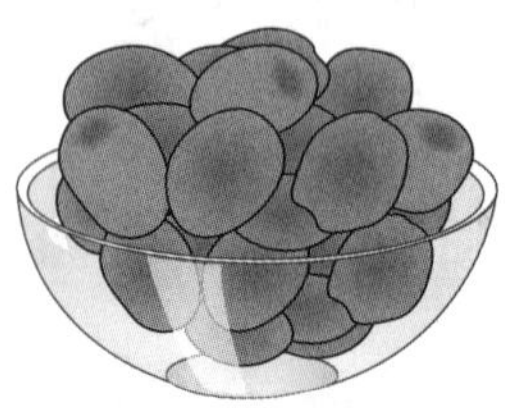
c

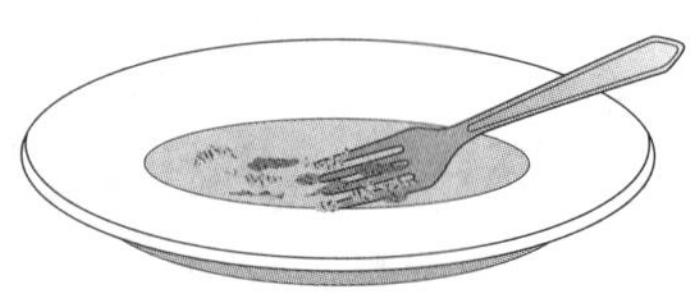
d

1. The olives are salty. ____
2. The cake was delicious. ____
3. The olives were salty. ____
4. The cake is delicious! ____

3 **Listen.** Read and circle. TR: 41

1. It looks beautiful.	It sounds beautiful.
2. It looks smooth.	It feels smooth.
3. No, there aren't any.	Yes, there are some.
4. Let's buy a loaf of bread.	Let's put away the loaf of bread.
5. No, there isn't any.	Yes, there is some in the bottle.
6. No, there isn't any.	Yes, there is a little.

4 **Read and write.** Use some words from the box.

are	Because	do	does	doesn't
don't	is	was	Why	

1. Why __________ lions eat bananas?
2. __________ lions eat meat.
3. How __________ the soda taste? It tastes sweet!
4. __________ does a zebra eat grass?
5. Why __________ the baby birds in the nest?
6. How __________ the soup? It was terrible!

5 **Read.** Check **T** for *True* and **F** for *False*.

1. A cat uses its tongue to drink. (T) (F)
2. A goat uses its horns to taste. (T) (F)
3. A parrot uses its wings to fly. (T) (F)

Unit 7

Feeling Fit

1 Look and write.

a back	a knee
a chest	a shoulder
an elbow	a stomach
fingers	toes

2 Circle the best answer.

1. I have ten **knees / elbows / fingers**.

2. I have two **shoulders / toes / backs**.

3. I have one **knee / muscle / stomach**.

4. I can bend my **bone / knees / chest**.

5. I can stretch my **knees / muscles / elbows**.

3 **Listen to the song.** Draw lines to match. **TR: 42**

1. Did you move your
2. Did you stretch your
3. Did you get enough
4. Did you eat a healthy
5. Did you stretch your
6. Did you touch your
7. Did you bend your
8. Did you wiggle your

a. sleep?
b. legs?
c. back?
d. snack?
e. nose?
f. muscles?
g. knees?
h. toes?

4 **Write a new verse for the song.** Use some words from the box.

chest	elbows	fingers	shoulders	stomach

Did you bend your ________________? Yes, I did!

Did you move your ________________? I did that a lot.

Did you touch your ________________? No, I forgot!

Did you stretch your ________________? Yes, I did.

GRAMMAR

Did you **eat** a snack?	Yes, I **did**.	
Did you **ride** your bike?	No, I **didn't**.	
Did she **do** her homework?	Yes, she **did**.	**didn't** = did not
Did he **make** his bed?	No, he **didn't.**	
Did they **go** for a walk?	Yes, they **did**.	
Did they **brush** their teeth?	No, they **didn't**.	

5 Listen and write. TR: 43

1. ________ you ________ your knees?
   Yes, I ________.
2. ________ she ________ in the park?
   Yes, she ________.
3. ________ you ________ breakfast?
   No, I ________.
4. ________ he ________ his back?
   No, he ________.
5. ________ they ________ their homework?
   No, they ________.

6 Listen and match. Draw lines. TR: 44

1. Did he walk to school?
2. Did you play baseball yesterday?
3. Did he brush his teeth after breakfast?
4. Did you play with friends yesterday?

a. Yes, I did.
b. Yes, he did.
c. No, I didn't.
d. No, he didn't.

7 **Look, read, and write.** Use *did* or *didn't* in your answers.

1. Did she throw the ball? Yes, she did.

2. Did he catch the ball? ____________________

3. Did the children ride their bikes to the park? ____________________

4. Did they eat the bread? ____________________

8 **Work with a partner.** Write questions. Ask your partner. Write the answers.

1. Did you eat yogurt for breakfast? ____________________

2. Did you ____________________? ____________________

3. Did you ____________________? ____________________

4. Did you ____________________? ____________________

5. Did you ____________________? ____________________

9 **Read and match.** Draw lines to match.

1. I eat vegetables at dinner.
2. I eat junk food on Saturday.
3. I eat fruit every morning.
4. I get rest every day.
5. I get exercise every day.
6. She eats fruit every day.
7. He eats junk food at night.
8. Why does he eat vegetables?
9. Does the baby get rest?
10. She gets exercise every day.

a. I like bananas and oranges.
b. I go to bed at 8:00.
c. I skateboard and rollerblade.
d. I love cookies and ice cream.
e. I like corn and peppers.
f. Because he loves them!
g. She loves mangoes.
h. She swims every afternoon.
i. He eats three bags of chips.
j. Yes. She sleeps at night.

10 **Look, read, and write.** Use words from the box.

eat fruit	eat junk food	eat vegetables	get exercise	get rest

1. They ________________ every day.

2. They ________________ every day.

GRAMMAR

It's important to get **enough** exercise. Don't watch **too** much TV.

I eat **enough** vegetables every day. I don't drink **too** much soda.

11 **Read.** Write *too* or *enough*.

1. Don't stay up ________ late!

2. I play soccer every day.

   I get ________ exercise.

3. Don't watch ________ much TV!

4. I drink ________ much soda.

12 **Read and write.** Answer the questions. Check ✓ *Yes* or *No*.

	Yes	No
1. Do you eat too much junk food?		
2. Do you get enough sleep at night?		
3. Do you play too many video games?		
4. Do you drink enough water every day?		
5. Do you eat enough fruit every day?		
6. Do you eat enough vegetables every day?		

13 **Work with a partner.** Student 1, go to page 123. Student 2, go to page 125. Take turns.

14 Do the word puzzle.

1. I like carrots. I eat enough v e g e t a b l e s.
2. I don't stay up too late. I get ☐☐☐☐☐☐ sleep.
3. Did she ☐☐☐☐☐ her teeth? Yes, she did.
4. ☐☐☐☐☐☐☐ your muscles.
5. I get enough ☐☐☐☐. I sleep at night.
6. I play soccer every day. I get enough ☐☐☐☐☐☐☐☐.
7. Wiggle your ☐☐☐☐☐☐☐.
8. ☐☐☐☐ your knees!
9. Did you go for a walk? Yes, I ☐☐☐.
10. Touch your ☐☐☐☐☐☐☐☐.
11. Don't eat too much ☐☐☐☐ ☐☐☐☐.
12. Bend your ☐☐☐☐☐.

15 Listen and read. Can you say these fast? TR: 45

1. Slowly stretch your stomach and shoulders on Sunday.
2. Eat enough fresh fruit every Friday.
3. Bonnie bends her beautiful back.

16 **Listen and read.** TR: 46

Do Animals Need Exercise?

Do animals get enough exercise? Wild animals do. They move a lot to look for food. They run, swim, climb trees, and walk far. Sometimes wild elephants walk more than twenty-seven miles (forty-five kilometers) a day!

Sometimes animals in zoos don't get enough exercise. They live in small spaces. Zookeepers always feed them. Many zookeepers help animals get exercise. At many zoos, the zookeepers teach elephants to stretch and bend. The elephants walk and run. They lift a heavy ball with their trunk. The zookeepers help big cats, like lions and tigers, too. A zookeeper hides a bone in a tree. Then the zookeeper teaches the big cats to climb and jump to get the bone. Big cats can also play with toys to stretch their muscles.

Sometimes pets don't get enough exercise. Dogs need to run outside. Cats need balls to hit with their paws. Birds need to flap their wings. It's important for pets to get enough exercise. Pet owners need to play with their pets. Exercise helps keep animals fit and healthy.

weird but true **An elephant's trunk can pick up one piece of grass, but it can also lift a big log.**

17 **Read.** Check **T** for *True* and **F** for *False*.

1. Wild animals get enough exercise. (T) (F)
2. Big cats pick up balls with their trunks. (T) (F)
3. Animals in zoos always get enough exercise. (T) (F)
4. Elephants in the wild walk a lot. (T) (F)
5. Exercise helps keep pets healthy. (T) (F)

18 **Read and write.** Complete the chart.

Animals and Exercise

	Do animals get enough exercise?	How do animals get exercise?
wild animals	______	They move a lot to look for food. They run, ______, ______, and ______.
zoo animals	sometimes	Zookeepers help animals get exercise. They teach elephants to ______ and ______ and lift a heavy ball. They teach big cats to ______ and ______ to get bones. Big cats play with toys.
pets	______	Pet owners ______. Dogs ______. Cats need to play with balls. Birds ______.

19 **Read and write.**

1. Why do wild animals get enough exercise?

______

2. How can zookeepers help elephants get enough exercise?

______

3. How can pet owners help their pets get enough exercise?

______

20 **Read and write.** Read about Gabriela's favorite vegetable. Underline the sentences with *because*. Write the words that tell why Gabriela likes tomatoes.

Tomatoes Are Great

My favorite vegetable is the tomato. I like tomatoes because they are juicy and delicious, and you can eat them hot or cold. You can cook tomatoes to make spaghetti sauce. You can eat them cold in salads. I also like tomatoes because they have beautiful colors! I love red, yellow, orange, and green tomatoes. I also like tomatoes because they help keep you healthy and strong.

____

____

____

21 **Write about your favorite vegetable or fruit.** Use *because* to explain why you like it.

____

____

____

____

____

22 **Read and write.** Use words from the box.

Did	didn't	Don't	rest
exercise	too	enough	

1. ________ she eat a snack yesterday? Yes, she did.

2. I get ____________ every day. I play basketball.

3. Do you get ____________ exercise? No, I watch _________ much TV.

4. Did you do your homework? No, I _________.

5. _________ eat too much junk food.

6. I get _________ every day. I go to sleep at 8:00.

23 **What's important for good health?** Read and check ✓. Compare answers with a partner. Are your answers the same?

	It's important for good health.
Get enough exercise every day.	
Eat fruits and vegetables.	
Eat junk food every day.	
Drink too much soda.	
Stretch your muscles.	
Stay up too late.	
Get enough rest.	
Drink enough water every day.	
Watch too much TV.	
Bend your knees and elbows.	
Eat foods to make your bones strong.	

Unit 8

Let's Celebrate!

1 Look and write.

a costume   a mask   a party   a feast   a lantern   a parade

celebrate   dance   decorations   remember   dress up   fireworks

1. ____________________

2. ____________________

3. ____________________

4. ____________________

5. ____________________

6. ____________________

7. ____________

8. ____________

9. ____________

10. ____________

11. ____________

12. ____________

2 Read and circle. Compare answers with a partner.

1. Do you like to dance?	Yes, I do.	No, I don't.
2. Do you like parties?	Yes, I do.	No, I don't.
3. Do you like to wear masks?	Yes, I do.	No, I don't.
4. Do you like to watch parades?	Yes, I do.	No, I don't.
5. Do you like feasts?	Yes, I do.	No, I don't.
6. Do you like decorations?	Yes, I do.	No, I don't.
7. Do you like lanterns?	Yes, I do.	No, I don't.
8. Do you like fireworks?	Yes, I do.	No, I don't.

3 **Listen to the song.** Read and write. TR: 47

1. We went to a carnival.

   Everyone was there!

   We dressed up, sang some songs,

   and watched a ______________.

2. Did you like the food?

   Yes, I liked the food.

   Did you ______________ ?

   Yes, I went as a frog.

3. Did you like the ______________ ?

   Yes, I liked the ______________.

   Did you see any ______________ ?

   Yes, we saw some ______________.

4 **Write a new verse for the song.** Use some words from the box.

dances	decorations	feast	fireworks	lanterns	party

Did you like the ________________________?

Yes, I liked the ________________________.

Did you see any ________________________?

Yes, I saw some ________________________.

GRAMMAR

Did you **watch** fireworks?	Yes, I **watched** fireworks.	**watched** = watch + ed
Did you **dress up**?	Yes, we **dressed up**.	**dressed** = dress + ed
Did you **like** the party?	Yes, I **liked** the party.	**liked** = lik~~e~~ + ed
Did your brother **dance**?	Yes, he **danced**.	**danced** = danc~~e~~ + ed

5 Listen and write. TR: 48

1. _____ you _________ to the party?

2. Yes, we _________ to the party.

3. _____ your cousins _________ with you?

4. Yes, they _________ with me.

5. _____ you _________ the yummy food?

6. Yes, I _________ the yummy food.

6 Read. Draw lines to match the questions to the answers.

1. Did you listen to music?
2. Did you watch fireworks?
3. Did you dress up in a costume?
4. Did you celebrate his birthday?
5. Did you like the feast?
6. Did you play games?

a. Yes, I dressed up in a costume.
b. Yes, I listened to music.
c. Yes, we celebrated his birthday.
d. Yes, I liked the feast.
e. Yes, we watched fireworks.
f. Yes, we played games.

7 Write these verbs so they tell about the past.

1. watch watched
2. listen ______
3. sound ______
4. cook ______
5. taste ______
6. celebrate ______
7. remember ______
8. brush ______

8 Read and write.

Complete the sentences. Use some verbs from Activity 7.

1. We ______ my brother's birthday yesterday.
2. My grandma ______ noodle soup.
3. The birthday feast ______ delicious.
4. We ______ to music and danced after dinner.
5. After we danced, we ______ a movie on TV.

9 **What about you?** What did you do on your birthday? Talk about what you did with a partner.

I played games on my birthday.

What games did you play?

1. I ______.
2. I ______.

10 **Look and read.** Draw lines to match.

balloons

a birthday cake

candles

a present

11 **Read.** Circle the best answer.

1. Today I'm nine years old. I have nine ____ on my birthday cake.

   a. presents b. invitations c. candles

2. My grandpa has ____ to my birthday party.

   a. an invitation b. a balloon c. a birthday cake

3. I have round ____ as decorations.

   a. presents b. balloons c. invitations

4. My ____ looks sweet and delicious!

   a. candle b. balloon c. birthday cake

5. Look at the picture. What's in the paper? It's a big ____ for me.

   a. candle b. invitation c. present

GRAMMAR

Did you **wear** a mask?	Yes, I **wore** a mask.
Did you **drink** soda?	Yes, I **drank** soda.
Did you **buy** her a present?	Yes, I **bought** her a present.

12 **Look at the gray words.** They are verbs. They change when you talk about the past. Match. Draw lines.

eat	rode	see	wrote
ride	had	write	saw
give	ate	drink	went
have	sang	go	drank
sing	took	wear	made
take	gave	make	wore

13 **Read and write.** Complete the sentences.

1. Did you write invitations? Yes, I ______ invitations.
2. Did you wear party hats? Yes, we ______ party hats.
3. Did your friends sing to you? Yes, my friends ______ to me.
4. Did you eat birthday cake? Yes, we ______ birthday cake.
5. Did you have fun? Yes, I ______ fun.

14 **Work with a partner.** Student 1, go to page 120. Student 2, go to page 126. Take turns.

15 **Read and write.** Do the crossword puzzle.

Down

1. I gave him a _____ on his birthday.
4. I don't _____ my third birthday, but I saw photos of it.
5. It was her eighth birthday, and she had eight _____ on her birthday cake.

Across

2. Did your sister wear a mask? Yes, she _____ a mask.
3. Did you sing a song? Yes, I _____ a song.
5. I wore a frog _____ to the party.
6. I saw the _____ in the sky. They were beautiful.
7. Did the children play games? Yes, they _____ games.
8. We _____ my birthday in May.
9. I was thirsty! I _____ the water.

16 **Listen and read.** Can you say these fast? **TR: 49**

1. Don't dance under the decorations!
2. Please pick up the purple party presents.
3. We celebrated and sang some songs slowly.

17 Listen and read. TR: 50

Celebrating the Sun

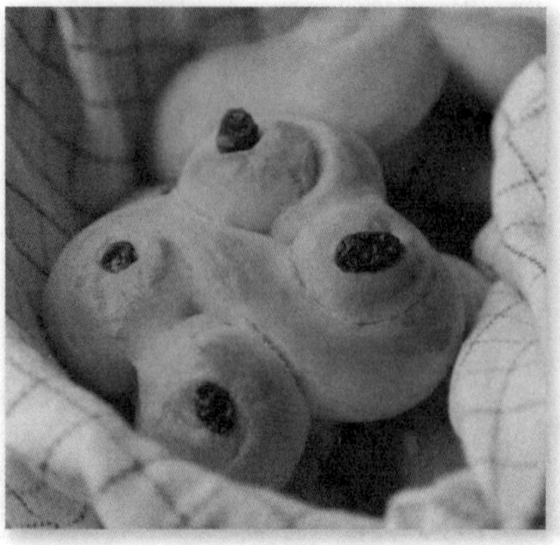

Many people all over the world celebrate the sun. Sweden is in the north. In winter, nights are long and days are short. On December 13, people celebrate Lucia Day. It is a festival of lights. People want light on long, dark days! Girls dress up as Lucia. They wear white dresses and wear a candle wreath on their head. Boys dress up as star boys. They wear white clothes and a white hat. They carry stars on sticks. The children sing songs, and people eat cookies and special sweet buns.

In Sweden, the festival of midsummer happens in June. Days are long, and nights are short. People celebrate the longest day of the year and the start of summer. People decorate their homes with flowers and leaves. Many people wear beautiful costumes to the festival. They dance and sing songs. They eat fish, potatoes, fruit, and other foods. People enjoy the sunlight and can forget about the cold, dark winter.

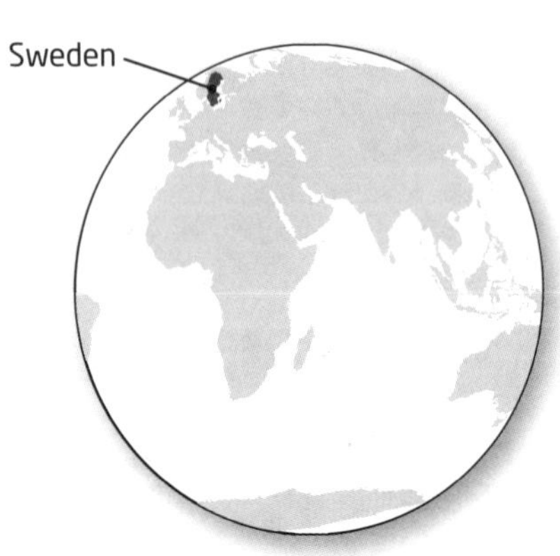

weird but true In the north of Sweden, it never gets dark at midsummer.

18 **Read.** Check **T** for *True* and **F** for *False*.

1. Lucia Day is a festival of stars. (T) (F)
2. Boys dress up as star boys on Lucia Day. (T) (F)
3. Girls wear candle wreaths on their head on Lucia Day. (T) (F)
4. The festival of midsummer is in December. (T) (F)
5. People dance and sing at the festival of midsummer. (T) (F)

19 **Work with a partner.** Read. Complete the chart.

	Lucia Day	Midsummer
When is it?		
What is it?	It is a festival of lights.	It is a festival to celebrate the longest day of the year and the start of summer.
What do people do?		

20 **Read and write.**

1. What do girls wear to dress up as Lucia?

____

2. What special food do people eat on Lucia Day?

____

3. What do people eat at the midsummer feast?

____

21 **Read.** Answer the questions. Write.

A Thanksgiving Day Parade

By Lisa

Every year there is a big parade in New York City on Thanksgiving Day. Thanksgiving is an American holiday. Last year we were in New York City, and I wanted to see the parade. It was cold, so I wore a warm coat and a hat. The parade was great! I listened to marching bands play music. I watched great dancers. My favorite things were big balloons shaped like animals!

1. What is the title of Lisa's writing? ______________________

2. What did Lisa wear? ______________________

3. What did Lisa hear? ______________________

4. What did Lisa see? ______________________

22 **Write about a parade or a party you went to.** Write a title for your paragraph. What did you wear? What did you see? What did you hear? What did you do?

____

By ____________

____

____

____

____

____

23 Read and draw.

1. Draw a birthday cake.
2. Draw candles on the cake.
3. Color the candles.
4. Draw a present next to the cake.

24 Listen and write. TR: 51

1. ______ you ______ to color the candles?
2. Yes, I ______.
3. Yes, I ______ my birthday.
4. Yes, they ______ me a present.
5. Yes, I ______ it.

25 Unscramble the sentences. Write.

1. Did / see / you / lanterns?

______

2. lanterns / I / saw / Yes,

______

3. wear / Did / a / mask? / you

______

4. mask / wore / a / I / Yes,

______

Unit 9

My Weekend

1 Look and write.

eat out go to the beach go to the movies go on a picnic
stay home text my friends visit a museum

1. ______________________

2. ______________________

3. ______________________

4. ______________________

5. ______________________

6. ______________________

7. ______________________

2 **Listen and write.** Use words from the box. TR: 52

busy exciting interesting lose win

1. I play soccer. I like to ______________.
2. I play games. I don't like to ______________.
3. The museum was ______________.
4. Last weekend, I was ______________. I had too much homework!
5. The parade was ______________.

3 **Work with a partner.** Ask and answer. Take turns.

Do you eat out on weekends?

Yes, I do.

4 **Listen to the song.** Read. Look. Draw lines to match. TR: 53

Did you go fishing?

Did you play baseball?

Did you go walking?

What did you do?

Did you go swimming?

Did you go hiking?

Did you go horseback riding?

5 **Listen.** Read and write. TR: 54

I __________ __________ fishing or walking.

I didn't __________ swimming or hiking.

I __________ a game with my little brother.

I __________ to the __________ with my mother.

GRAMMAR

How was your weekend?	It was boring. I **didn't have** fun.	**didn't** = did + not
What did you do?	I stayed home.	
What did your friends do?	They went to the movies.	
Did you text your friends?	No, I **didn't text** them.	

6 Listen and circle. TR: 55

1. I went to the movies. I went to the beach.
2. No, I didn't visit a museum. Yes, I visited a museum.
3. Yes, I went on a picnic. No, I didn't go on a picnic.
4. My team didn't win. My team won.
5. I had an interesting weekend! I had an exciting weekend!
6. Yes, we went to the movies. No, we didn't go to the movies.

7 **Read and match.** Draw lines.

1. How was your weekend?
2. Did your team win?
3. Did you eat out?
4. Did you go to the movies?
5. Did you visit a museum?
6. What did you do on Sunday?

a. No, I didn't go to the movies.
b. It was exciting. I went to the zoo.
c. No, they didn't win. They lost.
d. Yes, I did. I saw 100 paintings!
e. I flew in a helicopter.
f. No, we didn't eat out. We ate pizza at home.

8 **Read and write.** Complete the sentences. Use some words from the box.

didn't lose	didn't win	won	didn't stay
stayed	texted	didn't text	visited

1. I ______________ a museum. It was interesting.
2. I played soccer, but my team ______________. I was sad.
3. My family didn't eat out. We ______________ home and ate dinner.
4. I texted my friends, but they were busy and ______________ me.
5. My brother ______________ home after dinner. He went to the movies.

9 **What about you?** What did you do on the weekend? Read and write. Compare answers with a partner.

1. Did you fly a helicopter? (fly → flew)

   Yes, I flew a helicopter.

2. Did you do your homework?

   ____

3. Did you go on a picnic?

   ____

4. Did you stay home?

   ____

5. Did you text your friends?

   ____

6. Did you lose a game? (lose → lost)

   ____

10 **Look, read, and match.** Write the letter.

1. I go fishing in the river near my house. ______
2. My family likes to go hiking. ______
3. I go horseback riding on weekends. ______
4. I go ice skating in very cold weather. ______
5. I go swimming on hot days.

11 **Read and write.** Use words from the box.

go fishing	go hiking	go horseback riding
go ice skating	go swimming	

1. I ____________________ in summer at the swimming pool.
2. You have a horse! Do you ____________________?
3. It is very cold! I can ____________________.
4. I want fish for dinner. Let's ____________________.
5. I wear shoes and socks to ____________________. I walk and climb.

GRAMMAR

What **do** you **do** on weekends?	I usually **go swimming**.
What **did** you **do** last weekend?	I **went shopping**.
	I **didn't go swimming**.
What **does** he **do** on weekends?	He usually **goes fishing**.
What **did** he **do** last weekend?	He **didn't go fishing**.
	He **went running**.

12 **Look, read, and write.** Use *go* or *went* in your answers.

1. What did Mai do last weekend?
   She ______________________________.

2. What did her brother do last weekend?
   He ______________________________.
   What didn't Mai do?
   She ______________________________.

3. What did Ivan do last weekend?
   He ______________________________.

4. What did his sister do last weekend?
   She ______________________________.
   What didn't Ivan do?
   He ______________________________.

13 Listen and read. Circle. TR: 56

1. Olivia went horseback riding.	Olivia didn't go horseback riding.
2. She went bike riding.	She didn't go bike riding.
3. Olivia went skateboarding.	Olivia didn't go skateboarding.
4. Olivia went ice skating.	Olivia didn't go ice skating.
5. She went swimming.	She didn't go swimming.

14 **Work with a partner.** Student 1, go to page 123. Student 2, go to page 125. Take turns.

15 **Look, read, and write.** Answer the questions.

Monica

Miguel

Elena

Luis

1. What did Monica do on the weekend? She ______________________.
2. What did Luis do last weekend? He ______________________.
3. Did Elena go horseback riding? No, ______________________.
4. What did Elena do? She ______________________.
5. Miguel usually goes to the beach on weekends. What did Miguel do last weekend?

   He ______________________.

16 **Listen and read.** Can you say these fast? TR: 57

1. Why did we win the weekend game?
2. She went swimming and shopping on Saturday.
3. Bobby is busy at the beach.

17 **Listen and read.** TR: 58

Let's Go to the Aquarium!

Aquariums are great places to visit on the weekend. They teach us about oceans, rivers, wetlands, and other wet places. They teach us about plants and animals that live in water. You can see interesting ocean animals at many aquariums. Some aquariums have exciting things for children to do.

a beluga whale

The Shedd Aquarium in Chicago, USA, is very interesting. It has more than 32,500 animals! Turtles, frogs, and fish are some of the animals. Some of the fish are sharks. There are zebra sharks. Baby zebra sharks have stripes like a zebra! When some of the sharks are scared, they look like balloons. You can also see shark eggs at the aquarium!

a baby zebra shark

People can watch movies at the Shedd Aquarium. There are also many things for children to do. In the Polar Play Zone, children can wear a penguin costume and try to move like a penguin.

Aquariums are fun places to visit!

weird but true

You can take an elevator inside a really big aquarium in Germany. You can see more than 1,500 fish on your ride because the elevator is made of glass!

18 **Read.** Check **T** for *True* and **F** for *False*.

1. Aquariums are great places to go on weekends. (T) (F)
2. There are sharks at the Shedd Aquarium. (T) (F)
3. You can eat shark eggs at the Shedd Aquarium. (T) (F)
4. In the Polar Play Zone, you can dress up like a shark. (T) (F)
5. People can watch movies at the Shedd Aquarium. (T) (F)

19 **Read and write.** What's at the Shedd Aquarium? Complete the chart.

The Shedd Aquarium

Things I know are there	Things I think are there
zebra sharks	

20 **Work with a partner.** Ask and answer. Complete the chart.

	Me	My partner
1. Do you want to visit an aquarium?		
2. What do you want to see there?		
3. Why are aquariums interesting places to visit?		

21 Read and write. Read about Katya's busy afternoon. Underline the words that Katya uses to say when she did things.

1. What did Katya do first?

   She ______________________________

   __________________________________.

2. What did Katya do next?

   She ______________________________

   __________________________________.

3. Did Katya text her friends before or after she went shopping?

   She ____.

My Busy Afternoon

Last Saturday afternoon was busy! First, I went on a picnic with my family. Next, I played in a soccer game. I was happy because my team won! After that, I went shopping with my mom. I bought new shoes. Then I texted my friends, and we all went to a movie. After the movie, I went home. What a busy afternoon!

22 Write about a busy afternoon you had. Tell when you did things. Use words like *first, then, next,* and *after.*

23 **Unscramble the sentences.** Write.

1. did / last / do / weekend? / you / What

   ____

2. stayed / home. / I

   ____

3. We / go / ice skating. / didn't

   ____

4. baseball, / She / team / played / win. / her / didn't / but

   ____

5. fishing / We / river. / the / in / went

   ____

6. museum? / visit / a / you / Did

   ____

24 **Look at the pictures.** Read and write.

1. Did the dog go horseback riding?

   The dog ______________________.

2. What did the dog do last weekend?

   The dog ____________, ____________,

   and ____________.

25 **What about you?** What do you usually do on the weekend? Write.

I usually ______________________________

______________________________.

Review

1 Look and write.

2 Read and write. Use words from the box.

did didn't enough too

1. Did you eat vegetables yesterday? Yes, I ________________.
2. I drank five cans of soda! I drank ________________ much soda.
3. Did you eat junk food yesterday? No, I ________________.
4. I play basketball every day. I get ________________ exercise.
5. I go to bed at 8:30. I don't stay up ________________ late.
6. Did you stretch your muscles? Yes, I ________________.

3 **Read and write.** Complete the sentences.

1. Did you go to a party yesterday? Yes, I __________ to a party.
2. Did you celebrate Lupe's birthday? Yes, we __________ her birthday.
3. Did you eat birthday cake? Yes, we __________ birthday cake.
4. __________ you wear a costume? Yes, I __________ a cat costume.

4 **Read and look.** Draw lines to match.

1. What did you do last weekend?
   I went horseback riding.

2. What did you do on the weekend?
   I didn't go fishing.
3. What do you do on weekends?
   We usually visit a museum.

4. How was your weekend?
   It was OK. I stayed at home.
5. What did you do last weekend?
   We ate out.

5 **What about you?** Read and write.

1. Where did you go last weekend? ______________________________
2. What did you do before school? ______________________________

Unit 1 Student 1 Use with Activity 15 on page 10.

15 **Work with a partner.** Take turns. Look at the chart.

1. Ask your partner questions about Rosa and Carlos.
2. Listen to the answers.
3. Write the words in your chart.

What time does Carlos eat lunch?

Carlos sometimes eats lunch at twelve fifteen.

	eats lunch at 12:15 	comes home at 3:00 	has a snack at 3:30 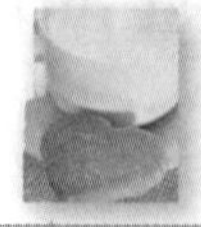	plays basketball at 4:45 	washes his/her pet snake at 6:00 
Rosa 	always		usually		never
Carlos 	sometimes	always		usually	

What time does Rosa eat lunch?

Rosa always eats lunch at twelve fifteen.

Unit 6 Student 1 Use with Activity 13 on page 72.

13 **Work with a partner.** Fill in the chart.

1. Look at the chart. Take turns asking and answering questions.
2. Write the questions and answers.

Is there any yogurt?

Yes, there is a little.

Questions	Answers
1. Is there any yogurt?	1. Yes, there is a little.
2. ______________________	2. No, there aren't any.
3. Are there any bags of chips?	3. ______________________
4. ______________________	4. No, there isn't any.
5. Is there any orange juice?	5. ______________________
6. ______________________	6. Yes, there is a little.
7. Are there any bottles of oil?	7. ______________________

Look at the completed chart. What foods do you need to buy?

____

Unit 2 Student 1 Use with Activity 11 on page 23.

11 Work with a partner.

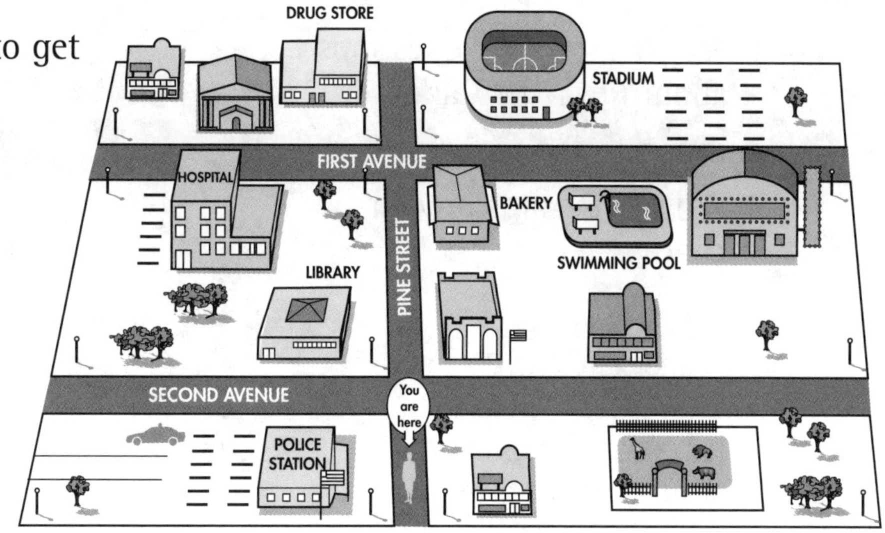

1. Ask your partner how to get to these places:
   toy store
   restaurant
   zoo
   movie theater
2. Follow your partner's directions.
3. Write the place names on the map.
4. Take turns asking and answering.
5. Look at your partner's map to check your answers.

Unit 4 Student 1 Use with Activity 14 on page 48.

14 Work with a partner. Fill in the chart.

1. Look at the chart. Take turns asking and answering questions.
2. Listen to your partner's questions and answers. Write them in the chart.
3. Check your partner's questions and answers.

Questions	Answers
1. How was the yogurt?	________________
2. ________________	They were salty.
3. How were the carrots?	________________
4. ________________	They were spicy.
5. How was the tea?	________________
6. ________________	It was sweet.

Unit 1 Student 2 Use with Activity 15 on page 10.

15 **Work with a partner.** Take turns. Look at the chart.

1. Ask your partner questions about Rosa and Carlos.
2. Listen to the answers.
3. Write the words in your chart.

What time does Carlos eat lunch?

Carlos sometimes eats lunch at twelve fifteen.

What time does Rosa eat lunch?

Rosa always eats lunch at twelve fifteen.

	eats lunch at 12:15 	comes home at 3:00 	has a snack at 3:30 	plays basketball at 4:45 	washes his/her pet snake at 6:00 
Rosa 	always	sometimes		always	
Carlos 	sometimes		never		never

Unit 8 Student 1 Use with Activity 14 on page 98.

14 **Work with a partner.** Take turns asking and answering questions. Listen to your partner's answers. Write them.

Questions	Write your answers	Answer your partner´s questions
1. Did Sara have a party?	1. ____________	1. He went to Sara's party.
2. Did her friends come to the party?	2. ____________	2. Yes, he rode his bike.
3. What did Sara's mom make?	3. ____________	3. He wore a bathing suit.
4. Did Sara take photos?	4. ____________	4. Yes, they swam at the party.
5. Did you see the photos?	5. ____________	5. He gave her a birthday present.

Unit 2 Student 2 Use with Activity 11 on page 23.

11 **Work with a partner.**

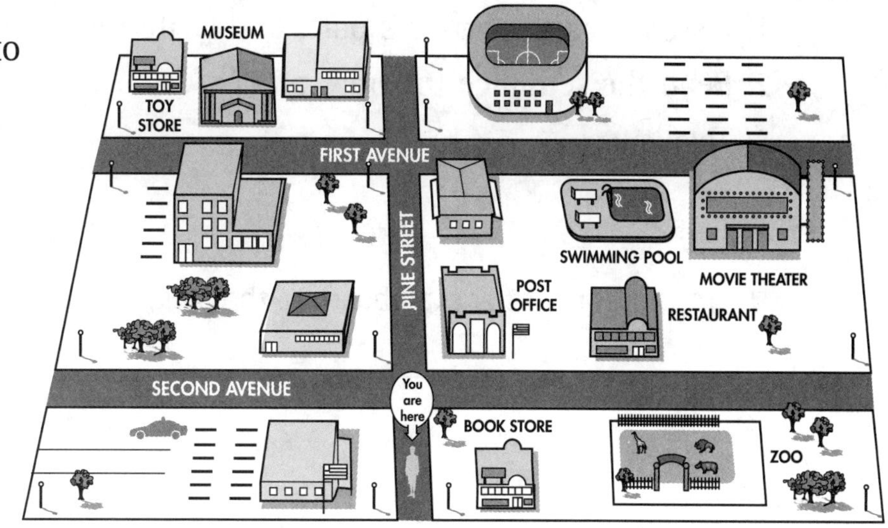

1. Ask your partner how to get to these places:
   stadium
   drug store
   library
   bakery
2. Follow your partner's directions.
3. Write the place names on the map.
4. Take turns asking and answering.
5. Look at your partner's map to check your answers.

Unit 4 Student 2 Use with Activity 14 on page 48.

14 **Work with a partner.** Fill in the chart.

1. Look at the chart. Take turns asking and answering questions.
2. Listen to your partner's questions and answers. Write them in the chart.
3. Check your partner's questions and answers.

Questions	Answers
1. ________________	It was sour.
2. How were the potato chips?	________________
3. ________________	They were delicious.
4. How were the red peppers?	________________
5. ________________	It was bitter.
6. How was the ice cream?	________________

Unit 3 Student 1 Use with Activity 13 on page 34.

13 **Work with a partner.** Read your part of the sentence.

1. Listen to your partner's part, and write the words.
2. Read the sentence to your partner.
3. Take turns.

1. My sister rides her skateboard to the park,

   ______________________________.

2. ______________________________,

   but the girl wants to play soccer.

3. The girl has cheese for a snack at 3:00,

   ______________________________.

4. ______________________________,

   but my sister wants to be an inventor.

5. He is laughing,

   ______________________________.

6. ______________________________,

   but the girl has a pet dog.

Unit 5 Student 1 Use with Activity 12 on page 60.

12 **Work with a partner.** Take turns. Read your part of each sentence. Listen to your partner's part. Write it. Read the sentences together.

1. Crocodiles use their sharp teeth ___to eat meat___.
2. ______________________________ to shower.
3. Butterflies use their wings ______________.
4. ______________________________ to fight.
5. Crocodiles use their long, strong tails ______________.

Unit 7 Student 1 Use with Activity 13 on page 87.

13 **Work with a partner.** Complete the paragraph.

1. Take turns reading sentences. Student 1 reads first.
2. Listen to your partner's part. Write the sentence.
3. Read the finished paragraph together.

I get enough exercise. ______________________________ I don't eat too much junk food. ______________________________ I drink enough water. ______________________________ Do you?

Unit 9 Student 1 Use with Activity 14 on page 111.

14 **Work with a partner.** Take turns asking and answering. Listen to your partner's answers. Write the answers to complete the chart.

	Ken's Weekend	Leo's Weekend
1. What does Ken usually do on weekends?		Leo usually goes fishing.
2. What did Ken do last Saturday?		Leo didn't go fishing. He went hiking.
3. What did Ken do last Sunday?		Leo went swimming.

Unit 3 Student 2 Use with Activity 13 on page 34.

13 **Work with a partner.** Read your part of the sentence.

1. Listen to your partner's part, and write the words.
2. Read the sentence to your partner.
3. Take turns.

1. ______________________________,

but my brother walks.

2. The boy wants to play baseball,

______________________________.

3. ______________________________,

but the boy has yogurt for a snack at 3:30.

4. My brother wants to be an artist,

______________________________.

5. ______________________________,

but she is crying.

6. The boy has a pet turtle,

______________________________.

Unit 5 Student 2 Use with Activity 12 on page 60.

12 **Work with a partner.** Take turns. Read your part of each sentence. Listen to your partner's part. Write it. Read the sentences together.

1. Crocodiles use their sharp teeth ________ to eat meat.
2. Elephants use their long trunks ________.
3. ________ to fly.
4. Sheep use their horns ________.
5. ________ to swim.

Unit 7 Student 2 Use with Activity 13 on page 87.

13 **Work with a partner.** Complete the paragraph.

1. Take turns reading sentences. Student 1 reads first.
2. Listen to your partner's part. Write the sentence.
3. Read the finished paragraph together.

________ I don't watch too much TV. ________ ________ I eat enough vegetables. ________ I get enough rest. Do you?

Unit 9 Student 2 Use with Activity 14 on page 111.

14 **Work with a partner.** Take turns asking and answering. Listen to your partner's answers. Write the answers to complete the chart.

	Ken's Weekend	Leo's Weekend
1. What does Leo usually do on weekends?	Ken usually goes swimming.	________
2. What did Leo do last Saturday?	Ken didn't go swimming. Ken went ice skating.	________ ________
3. What did Leo do last Sunday?	Ken went horseback riding.	________

Unit 6 Student 2 Use with Activity 13 on page 72.

13 **Work with a partner.** Fill in the chart.

1. Look at the chart. Take turns asking and answering questions.
2. Write the questions and answers.

Is there any yogurt?

Yes, there is a little.

Questions	Answers
1. Is there any yogurt?	1. Yes, there is a little.
2. Are there any jars of olives?	2. ___
3. ___	3. Yes, there are a few.
4. Is there any milk?	4. ___
5. ___	5. No, there isn't any.
6. Is there any meat?	6. ___
7. ___	7. No, there aren't any.

Look at the completed chart. What foods do you need to buy?

___

Unit 8 Student 2 Use with Activity 14 on page 98.

14 **Work with a partner.** Take turns asking and answering questions. Listen to your partner's answers. Write them.

Questions	Write your answers	Answer your partner´s questions
1. Where did Hugo go?	1. ___	1. Yes, she had a party.
2. Did Hugo ride his bike to the party?	2. ___	2. Yes, they came to the party.
3. What did Hugo wear?	3. ___	3. She made a feast!
4. Did people swim at the party?	4. ___ ___	4. No, her dad took photos.
5. What did Hugo give Sara?	5. ___ ___	5. Yes, I saw them.